The Art of Successful Information Systems Outsourcing

The Art of Successful Information Systems Outsourcing

David Gefen

business**expert**
Press

The Art of Successful Information Systems Outsourcing
Copyright © Business Expert Press, LLC, 2010.

First published in 2010 by
Business Expert Press, LLC
222 East 46th Street, New York, NY 10017
www.businessexpertpress.com

ISBN-13: 978-1-60649-161-4 (paperback)
ISBN-13: 978-1-60649-162-1 (e-book)

DOI 10.4128/9781606491621

A publication in the Business Expert Press Information Systems
collection

Collection ISSN: 2156-6577 (print)
Collection ISSN: 2156-6593 (electronic)

Cover design by Jonathan Pennell
Interior design by Scribe Inc.

First edition: December 2010

10 9 8 7 6 5 4 3 2 1

Printed in the United States of America.

Abstract

As with other pressing issues of information systems (IS) management, managing IS outsourcing also began as a solution to industry needs, and much of this book is accordingly based on industry experience cloaked as it were in academic theory garb to add depth to these proven practices as well as allow for borrowing insight from other academic disciplines.

With this approach in mind, after a quick review of what IS outsourcing is in chapter 1 and its topology in chapter 2, the book delves into this technology imperative as a core driver of IS outsourcing beyond the cost savings aspect central in other types of outsourcing, in chapter 3. The technology imperative explains why IS outsourcing is also as much about acquiring capabilities that cannot be quickly acquired or indeed planned for in advance because of the revolutionary advances in technology. This unique perspective on IS outsourcing also makes it unique from other types of outsourcing, and the remainder of the book addresses these unique issues from a head-on practitioner perspective while adding a broader theoretical perspective.

It is this uniqueness of IS management that also makes the search for a boilerplate methodology that may apply across scenarios as futile as searching for a silver bullet. Nonetheless, attaining the correct mind-set is essential and is the first step in managing IS outsourcing. The lack of such a mind-set is in many cases the cause for the reported high failure rate in IS outsourcing. Knowing yourself and knowing your enemy, as Sun Tsu taught, and knowing the terrain, too—and accordingly adopting a mind-set of identifying and managing risks—are all crucial. This mind-set is what makes for successful IS outsourcing.

Keywords

IT and IS outsourcing, Cloud computing, technology imperative, user push toward outsourcing, outsourcing mind-set, understanding the stakeholders, outsourcing topology, outsourcing risk management, vendor psychology, the contracting process, internal resistance

Contents

Prologue

The idea for this book started when I was sitting with the CIO (chief information officer—the senior executive in charge of the information systems [IS] and information technology [IT] services) of one of the largest second-tier suppliers to the automotive industry outside Detroit. The man said at the time that his company outsources their IT and IS on a regular basis, but he has no idea if he is doing it correctly. Subsequent talks with other CIOs confirmed this observation. Companies outsource their IT and IS but are really uncertain whether they are doing so correctly. Indeed, in reading many practitioner books on the subject, it is hard to escape the feeling that managers do it, and know how to do it right most of the time, but they only see things head on. They see the dots. This book is about connecting these dots into a pattern by weaving them together through the perspective of theory.

What makes this book special is that it focuses on down-to-earth practical advice gleaned from the experience of dozens of senior IT project managers and CIOs and so deals with outsourcing on a practical level, but it also complements this with a theoretical academic view showing the pattern in the dots. The book does not hide the real complexity of the issue and does not attempt to introduce the reader to some elusive nonexistent boilerplate solution. Instead, the book treats outsourcing for what it is: a complex issue with no silver bullet—but where, nonetheless, steps can be taken to understand outsourcing for what it is and manage the process accordingly and know when to avoid it altogether. It is this focus on the correct mind-set, rather than methodology steps alone, that makes this book unique. The book is written for managers, students, and academics involved in and studying outsourcing. This book is about coaching the reader about managing the outsourcing of information systems, not necessarily about offshoring them, and in doing so complement existing books and research.

A convenient way to image this complexity and the ways to address it is to think of an IT outsourcing project as an iceberg. You, the skipper, are happily sailing the big blue sea when you suddenly see this iceberg. Realizing things for what they are, you try to avoid the dangers while taking advantage of the opportunities. This is the correct thing to do, and to some extent you can do it. But the real danger lies in the 90% part of the iceberg that is submerged and that you do not see unless you happen to be simultaneously flying overhead with an airborne sonar system. And even then, the real risks are still there unless you know what immanent dangers to measure. This book is designed to address this dual perspective by combining the practices of managing outsourcing as seen by managers in the field facing this iceberg head-on on the one hand, with a proverbial 30,000-foot academic water-piercing sonar perspective on the other— and, in doing so, to introduce the reader to a unique blend of head-on manager insights and academic theory.

We see further because we stand on the shoulders of those who came before us and those who hold us up now. So, many thanks are due to the many people whom I have worked with in the past, to many CIOs who shared their current experiences with me and my colleagues, and especially to my wife.

CHAPTER 1

What It Is All About

故曰：知彼知己，百戰不殆；不知彼而知己，一勝一負；不知彼，不知己，每戰必殆

—Sun Tsu[1]

Overview of IS Outsourcing

Outsourcing is about letting out work that might have been done in-house to another company, with all the benefits and *risks* such a step entails. This book is about coaching the reader in the management of a special kind of outsourcing, that of information systems (IS) and information technology (IT).[2] In the interest of brevity we shall refer to both contexts as IS outsourcing because of the overlap in risk analyses in both.

The decision to outsource IS development, service, or maintenance is often a crucial one because in many organizations IS strategy and organizational strategy are two sides of the same coin. Information systems through information technology integrate and standardize the organization and its operations. IS provide the bottom-up information flow from the employees who service the customer or manufacture the goods to senior management who, thanks to IS, can have a real-time picture of exactly what is happening and where. And, most importantly, IS provide the top-down command and control structure through which senior management determines what these employees can and cannot do by enforcing organizational policy and work flow in a manner unattainable without IS. It is because of this symbiotic relationship that strategic IS decisions are often strategic organizational decisions and that strategic organizational decisions depend on IS to be fulfilled. In fact, the symbiosis between the organization and its IS is such that IS are often described as the nervous system of the organization.[3] Outsourcing the nervous system may have its benefits and, as we shall discuss, may be necessary and sometimes even an unavoidable consequence of the technology and its rapid evolution, but it is risky. And that leads to the theme of this book:

The key to successful IS outsourcing is to know these risks and to take the right steps to control them.

As you read the book you may say to yourself, "But in my company this is not how we did it." That may indeed be the case. Things differ across organizations because of project characteristics, because of IT maturity levels, because projects are born and borne differently, and so on. Still, at a higher level of abstraction, a proverbial 30,000-foot view, there are many parallels to why outsourcing projects do and do not succeed. And so, although there is no silver bullet because every project, technology, team, requirements, vendor, company, risks, and so on are unique, there is a correct and mostly recurring mind-set when these projects do make it. This book is about these overall principles as seen at this proverbial 30,000-foot view.

What you need to remember as you read this book is that outsourcing is about allocating the risks and responsibilities to another company. It is about having someone else do something for you because they can do it cheaper, faster, or better, for example, by reusing their expertise to gain economies of scale.[4] Outsourcing is *not* about abrogating your responsibility or externalizing internal headaches such as a malfunctioning IT department.

As we progress through the book we shall discuss these risks in ever increasing circles, starting with the risks of not understanding what outsourcing is and what it is not in this chapter. We shall then discuss the risks related to the evolution of the technology, and specifically to the maturity of the way the organization uses its IS in view of the diffusion of innovation theory[5] in chapter 3, progressing through the need to recognize and address risks in one's own company before taking any steps toward outsourcing outside the realm of the company in chapters 4 and 5.

Even if you the reader are not directly interested in IS outsourcing management but you are interested in outsourcing in other contexts, you should consider reading this book because what applies to IS applies to other industries too—except that IS move so much faster, with a new technology with revolutions every 5 years or so and new technologies every 1.5 to 2 years. Indeed, as you read the book you will probably see the parallels with other high-tech industries such as pharmaceuticals.

The Ubiquity of IS Outsourcing

Indeed, IS outsourcing, with its increased benefits and risks, is all around us. It is unavoidable. Although it may be unknown to you, you too are probably already outsourcing with what is currently called Cloud computing or SaaS computing (SaaS, standing for software as a service, is the current buzz word for what used to be called application service providers, or ASP, some time ago). When you use Gmail and Google Docs instead of the e-mail and word-processing applications, respectively, that come with Microsoft Office on your PC, or when you use TurboTax on the web instead of as an application you install on your laptop, or when you use Lala.com to access music on the web wherever you are instead of the limited service iTunes gives you only on your own PC—in all these cases you are technically outsourcing the IS services you are using.[6] And you are not alone. Several universities have already decided to adopt Gmail as their standard e-mail service, thus cutting their expenses while increasing the quality and uptime of their service. Google's new operating system Chrome OS will take this common experience of outsourcing to the next stage: even your operating system will be mostly outsourced and in the process might even be better, certainly cheaper (well, it is free), automatically updateable, and, importantly, mostly on a remote server of which you are totally unaware. Having all this on a remote server has the distinct advantage of saving you or your company the headache, and considerable cost, of upgrading the CPU and memory and key applications every time a new operating system or other resource-devouring software you are dependent on is released. Outsourcing IS services has its benefits. And just as it is beneficial to you as an individual, so it can be beneficial to organizations, providing, in both cases, that it is outsourced while you and your company realize what the risks are and take appropriate steps to control these risks.

It should come as no surprise, then, that IS outsourcing is growing at an incredible speed, according to some industry reports attributed to Gartner assessing the worldwide IT outsourcing services. These reports include IS, at $806 billion in 2008, an increase of 8.2% over 2007, with IBM, HP, and Accenture holding the top market-share positions.[7] Already in 2005, 95% of *Fortune* 1000 companies outsourced, although most of them only selectively, while among smaller companies outsourcing took on a much slower rate with only 19% of companies outsourcing, according to Dominguez.[8] Average cost savings all together stands at an average of about 10%, although in 28% of the companies the result was actually increased costs[9] A chief information officers' (CIO) roundtable I attended in Detroit in 2009 confirmed this pattern: Larger companies tend to outsource more, the smaller ones do not, and all emphasized that cost savings, provided the outsourcing is done correctly, is probably around the 10% mark only and not the 40% mark some vendors claim. Indeed, in a survey the consulting firm Deloitte published,[10] in which they studied some of the companies in the *Fortune* 500 listing, they found that outsourcing is fraught with risks and that although 70% of the companies outsourced to save costs, 38% of those incurred hidden costs that cut into their expected profits. The reason for this, adds Deloitte, is that outsourcing is a very complex process and that its risks cannot be completely mitigated. Still, 30% of the world's largest 1,000 firms already outsourced offshore by 2005.[11]

The Lack of a Boilerplate Solution to IS Outsourcing

There is no boilerplate methodology for IS outsourcing. There are mistakes you can learn to avoid by a risk-conscious mind-set, but the truth is that outsourcing IS projects successfully is overwhelmingly complex unless you stick to very standardized types of services such as Gmail. To demonstrate this complexity, imagine a medium-sized IS project. This type of project will be based on a requirements document, which even in a small IS project may span over 5,000 pages. My experience as a systems analyst and project manager leads me to be skeptical of how many people actually read all the pages of such a document, let alone try to identify potential overlaps and conflicts within it. Seeing all the conflicting details and missing pieces just from reading the requirements document is impossible, even among the few, including the project manager and systems analysts, who do try to do so. This complexity in developing IS projects can be likened to a large puzzle. One never knows if pieces are missing or are not cut correctly around the corners until one puts almost all the puzzle together—except that a large IS has many more pieces than the several hundred of a jigsaw puzzle. Now, when the IS project is managed inside the company many of these issues of missing or wrongly defined software modules, the equivalent of the proverbial jigsaw puzzle pieces, can be more easily resolved—albeit industry numbers have been putting in-house (in-house means developing and maintaining the IS inside the organization, rather than outsourcing it) IS project failure rates at around 30% for years.[12] Add to this complexity the additional distance between developers and users that outsourcing brings, and add to this the fact that the outsourcing client cannot go back and change the details because a contract is a contract, and the consequences of outsourcing makes the management of such IS projects so much more complex. It is in fact so complex that economic theory has not yet converged on a proper way to manage this.[13] Indeed, the failure rate in IS outsourcing is estimated by Gartner at around 50%.[14]

There may be no boilerplate, but there is a correct mind-set: Treat outsourcing as an iceberg. With an iceberg one sees lots of serious dangers and one may be able to navigate around them, but the real danger lies in the submerged part. It is because one never quite sees the whole picture that it is imperative to treat the risks with the utmost respect. Nonetheless, because IS outsourcing is here to stay, this book does provide at the end of this chapter a tentative boilerplate guideline to assist the reader in trying to steer away from the iceberg. This is important because it is estimated that only about 10% of IS outsourcing contracts actually save money,[15] while in most cases—according to industry surveys—companies have had second thoughts about outsourcing their IS and have decided to bring it back in-house.[16] Although there is no silver bullet because every project, technology, team, requirements, vendor, company, risks, and so on are unique, there is a correct and mostly recurring mind-set. The tentative boilerplate is geared to create awareness in that direction.

The Driving Forces Behind IS Outsourcing

There are many driving forces in the marketplace that contribute to why outsourcing is becoming so prevalent and unavoidable. Among the more common reasons, which we shall review in this chapter, are (a) the escalating costs of IS development combined with limited resources; (b) the limited availability of high-quality staff; and (c) the ready availability of standardized packages. Let's examine these one at a time.

Escalating Costs

A key problem CIOs have is the need to do more with less. Many U.S. and European companies face budget freezes, including a freeze on hiring new IS staff, coupled with the need to continue maintaining services on existing IS. According to some reports, already 70% of IS budget goes to maintenance.[17] This means most of the budget goes to managing and supporting existing systems. This gives IS managers very little wiggle room in financing new IS, although the need is clearly there. Without the ability to hire new staff, but still being compelled to provide new services, there is little wonder many CIOs outsource either the development of new IS or the maintenance of their legacy systems so they can release their staff to develop new systems. Outsourcing is the answer.

This need to do more with less is compounded by shrinking IT budgets. The average IT budget as a percent of company revenue declined from a high of 3.88% in 2001 to only 2.80% in 2008.[18] Combine this with evidence that industry concentration (the market share held by the top 20 largest firms) is growing, especially among high-IT companies and that the composition of these top 20 companies annually changes more in high-IT companies, and that the performance in gross profit margin between the 25th percentile and the 75th percentile is growing "dramatically,"[19] and the obvious imperative to outsource is at least partly there.

Outsourcing in theory allows CIOs to get things done faster and cheaper. Importantly, it also allows CIOs to deliver new IS without the need to hire a lot of new personnel to build the new IS and then fire many of them when it is ready. Hiring and firing are expensive financially and emotionally, and these are not things CIOs want to spend all their time doing. CIOs can rely instead on outsourcing, especially as software and its related services have become considerably more standardized and integrated over the years. Indeed, as a CIO in Phoenix, Arizona, told me in December 2009, he often has to outsource simply because he does not have the personnel to develop necessary IS otherwise. Important for the next chapters, this CIO also added that when he does outsource he explains to his IT group that he is going to outsource because, even if they worked overtime, they could not complete the tasks on time.

The market imperative to support outsourcing is there, too. Customizing an enterprise resource planning (ERP) system or developing a website requires a lot of initial learning, representing substantial setup costs, but customizing subsequent ERP systems or building other websites once the first one has been done correctly is substantially cheaper. As a result, a vendor has economies of scales in providing these services. The vendor can deliver the new IS at a considerably cheaper price and much faster. Moreover, since the vendor has already done so many times in the past, the vendor can promise a reliable delivery schedule, something an in-house team developing such a system for the first time cannot so easily do. And, no less important in the context of software projects, the software the vendor will be delivering will probably be of higher quality, even if it does not include all kinds of additional, unstandardized features the in-house team may add.

Availability of High-Quality Staff

Such an outsourcing vendor will also have the advantage of already having the trained staff it needs. Software vendors tend to specialize in specific topics, and this is what gives them the advantage of economies of scale. Specializing in this manner allows these vendors to search and then hire the experts they need for these specialties. This is an important consideration because these experts are not readily available, and when they are, their salaries might be out of proportion to what other employees in the client company make. The experts too have an incentive to prefer working for a vendor. With technology moving at an ever increasing speed, expertise becomes obsolete unless one continually keeps up to date, and it is easier to keep up to date when working with many other experts in related fields and when your company specializes in selling your expertise and is therefore more open to sending you to expensive conferences and courses. This concentration of expertise creates value for the experts and gives the vendors an advantage in hiring them. Moreover, having a large team of such experts work together gives the vendor the necessary backup in case one of these experts is not available, and, more so, these experts reinforce the expertise of each other by sharing best practices and helping each other out in the case of harder problems.

All these are benefits a small company cannot afford to have, but can have access to should it rely on an outsourcing vendor. Outsourcing can make these experts available to the client without the high costs of seeking them (typically this amounts to at least one month's salary to the recruiting firm)—assuming of course that the client knows what specific expertise it needs, which is not always the case. Moreover, by acquiring the services of the outsourcing vendor the client need only pay for the time or task it needs the experts for rather than paying them a very high salary regularly for work that is only infrequently needed. A regular company that does not have a very large IT staff cannot afford, and indeed does not need, many such experts.

Availability of Standardized Packages

Another process contributing significantly to the growth of IS outsourcing is the standardization of IS services and the increasing reliance on interindustry standards.[20] If one were to map the evolution of software and its computer sciences philosophy one would notice a trend toward increased standardization and integration of IS both in the industry at large and within companies. If in the 1960s and 1970s companies developed proprietary software and hardware that would not connect to the software or hardware of other companies, the trend today is the exact opposite: Everything is supposed to be "plug-and-play," and uniform standards rule. In fact, a driving force behind software development is the "object-oriented" approach, which is precisely about allowing such interconnectivity. The growth of open source software, such as the Linux operating systems, plays into this theme, too.[21] The trend began in the early 1980s with the advent of the IBM PC. At that time IBM's decision to acquire hardware and software from other companies to install in their new computer was unheard of. As we shall discuss in chapter 3, this market move toward open source and plug-and-play connections has had a dramatic effect on market segmentation and on the speed at which companies need to respond to new technologies and the business opportunities these new technologies create. With the market evolving so quickly and with few companies able to master every new technology, it becomes an imperative to rely on contracting out part of the work to other companies.

This trend toward standardization and integration applies also within organizations. As several CIOs in the automotive industry in Detroit told my colleagues and I at a roundtable we organized, integration of their IS is a key IS policy within their organizations. From an outsourcing perspective, this standardization is borne out in several important aspects. First, within organizations both the IT infrastructure and the IS programs run on this infrastructure are being forced by organizational policy to be standard. It is the same e-mail system, the same ERP, the same communication network, and so on throughout the organization. This allows for easier management and for economies of scale. It also means fewer interconnectivity problems. Users are not only discouraged from using proprietary software but also in some cases actually forbidden to do so as the IT department strives to achieve interconnectivity among the many IT platforms and software systems it runs.

We also see this standardization with the continued and increasing emergence of quality certificates in the software industry. A leader in this process of standardization is the Software Engineering Institute at Carnegie Mellon University and their capability maturity model integrated (CMMI) standard.[22] CMMI is a quality certificate of the software development process. It is widely used around the world with many leading software vendors boasting of having reached level 5, the highest level in CMMI, because of the reputation it entails.[23] Indeed, every one of the 30 leading Indian software outsourcing companies has CMMI maturity level 5, and this gives them a distinct advantage over Chinese companies.[24]

Closely related to this is the growing availability of standardized packages (e.g., SAP), which make it cheaper and faster to purchase ready-made IS and standardized customization, rather than develop things in-house. In fact, nobody today, with the possible exception of Google, develops their own proprietary word processor. It makes no sense. Developing such complex IS in-house requires an enormous investment and extensive expertise. Acquiring the service for free on Google Docs or even paying several hundred dollars to buy it from Microsoft is so much cheaper, faster, and probably better, that it makes no sense to hire expert programmers to develop it in-house. This was not always the case. Back in the 1970s it was not uncommon for companies to develop their own proprietary databases. This increasing reliance on available standardized packages has become one of the dominant trends in the software industry.[25] In fact, *The Economist*[26] claims that start-up banks are using outsourcing as a way to leapfrog their IT ahead of the IT of many of the established banks they compete with who are still straddled with their 1960s-era mainframe applications.

This drive toward standardization of everything IS and IT makes it so much easier to outsource. The prospect and need to develop and maintain IS in-house becomes less necessary and cost justified.

Other Reasons Companies Choose to Rely on IS Outsourcing

Companies outsource their IS services for a variety of reasons. Three of the main reasons, in a progression of IS outsourcing maturity, are cutting costs, acquiring resources, and forming alliances.[27] More on this transition in the following chapters. Here we shall discuss these three reasons.

Cutting Costs

Outsourcing is at least partly a business question, and like any business question the bottom line is always literally and figuratively the bottom line. A primary reason companies outsource is to cut costs. Hiring another company to do the work your company does at a lower cost is a valid and important business consideration. For example, outsourcing may lead to cutting payroll costs, a euphemism for layoffs, and that may cut costs. One should be aware, however, that the risks this entails may also carry a high price tag and that this price tag may cause these expected cost savings to not materialize. In the short term this may seem to cut costs, but in the long term it may also result in low morale and lost expertise and knowledge, and making up for these may end up costing more than was saved.

As an IS project manager one wants to be especially cautious about this. Most IS projects fail not because of the technology but because of people issues, mainly their resistance to adopting the new IS. *Any IS, no matter how good it is, if it is not used, is useless;* and the primary reason IS are not used is because of people problems. Therefore, as an IS manager one should want to be cautious about layoffs or even the implication of layoffs.[28] In fact, in one of the larger projects I took part in where I was a manager on the outsourcing vendor's side, we and the management of the client organization made it a point to clarify to the client's employees that they would not lose out because of the outsourcing of the project to us and that they would certainly not lose out because of the new IS being implemented. The outsourcing project and the implementation of the IS through it were deliberately managed to make it a win-win situation for everybody, and it was done so precisely to avoid user resistance. And in the few cases where the client employees were skeptical of how truly this policy would be carried out by their management we encountered quite a bit of user resistance to the new IS, at least until the policy bore itself out and these employees were convinced that the new IS would not be counterproductive to their interests. This is all about managing trust, a topic we shall discuss more in the following chapters. At least from an IS management perspective, saving costs through outsourcing but at the cost of alienating employees is not always a good idea.

When it comes to cutting costs through outsourcing, companies sometimes expect savings in the unrealistic realm of a 20% to 40% cost-saving margin, so industry experts such as Ashley[29] claim. These numbers about outsourcing in general are consistent with the numbers CIOs give me at roundtables. These numbers are not realistic in the long term. The vendor may be able to cut costs relative to the client because of economies of scale and because it can employ people in countries with cheaper labor costs, but the outsourcing vendor must also make a profit, and a 40% cost cut does not leave the vendor with much profit. The client may be able to force such cost-cutting margins on a vendor, but beware, the old saying that you get what you pay for applies equally well in outsourcing, too.

I was personally involved on the vendor's side in several projects where the client tried to force cost cutting. The inevitable result was less quality control testing by the vendor and the loss of additional features that would have been thrown in by the vendor free of charge had the vendor not been forced to work on a shoestring budget. Moreover, in those cases where we identified missing necessary features in the requirements—and we identified these earlier than the client could have because we tested the software before the client got it and because we saw the mismatched proverbial puzzle pieces as we were building them—our senior management was not at all eager to let us add those missing features to the software (something we would have normally done) because they reckoned we were already losing too much money on this project. This was a mistake the client made. In software projects it is close to impossible to get the requirements right the first time around. This has always been the case.[30] Once a project is completed the developer and the client suddenly realize how many things were excluded from the requirements or wrongly specified. This is to be expected. No one actually sees the whole picture in a 5,000-page requirements document. This is not a unique case. The literature is replete with stories about how requirements in outsourcing contracts are incomplete.[31] The client in this case may have been penny-wise in saving costs here and there but was also dollar stupid, having to pay through the nose for these additional features originally not part of the contract once it became clear that the project would not succeed without them. This ended up as a classic case of the vendor having a lock-in on the client and pressing this advantage to charge above market price accordingly. Had the client not insisted on forcing the vendor to cut costs to such an extreme, these additional features would have been thrown in free of charge. After all, the vendor knows the requirements are not perfect and so takes a safety margin in the price it bids so it can include minor modifications without charging the client. The vendor wants to see the project succeed as well but will not go broke for this. Cutting costs by the client should be done with the vendor's reaction in mind.

Another reason a high cost-savings rate may be unrealistic is that it takes the vendor time to come up to speed. The vendor may have cheaper operating costs because of its expertise and economies of scale, and perhaps cheaper labor abroad, and a 10% to 20% cost savings is possible (so I am told by CIOs I talk to), but those cheaper costs apply only after the vendor is already fully versed in what needs to be done. Initially, the vendor will need to learn the client organization and how it operates. These start-up costs will bite into the profits the vendor can expect to make and will accordingly result in lower cost savings for the client. Basically, out-sourcing IS does hold the promise of cutting costs, but things are seldom as rosy as they are hyped and hoped to be.

It is worth remembering the following adage in this context: *You get what you pay for.* In the long run, companies compete on quality and uniqueness, not on cheaper cost.[32] That is why, in the bank we studied,[33] bids that were not closely within the bank's project managers' estimated range were ignored outright. The same, I was told by CIOs I spoke to, applies in other companies, too. The lowest bid is not necessarily the cho-sen bid. Interestingly, also in online software markets (OSM) we stud-ied,[34] bidding lower than others is also no guarantee of having your bid chosen. In fact, seldom is the lowest bid the one chosen. What counts in both cases are trustworthiness indicators (more on that topic in the fol-lowing chapters). That lower costs should not be the guiding principle makes perfectly good business sense, too. The cost of a glitch in IS is not measured primarily in terms of the time it takes to correct it but rather in terms of the damage it causes—lost business, corrupt data, lost repu-tation, government fines, and so on. Brought into perspective, cutting costs through outsourcing or otherwise may be an imperative because the bottom line is literally always the bottom line, meaning that without a positive cash flow any company is in deep trouble. But the vendor also wants and needs to make a profit, and as we shall discuss in the follow-ing chapters it is in the interest of the client as well that the vendor is happy, and this eventually leads to increased costs. Indeed, we see this with the Indian IS outsourcing vendor market where first-tier, that is, high-quality, providers are not so cheap any more compared with their American or European rivals.

As a rule, basing a company's entire IS outsourcing strategy on costs alone might be unwise in the long term because, once the vendor creates a lock-in, the price might go up,[35] and, as I can testify from my own expe-rience on the vendor side and as noted by other research,[36] service quality might go down.

Acquiring Expertise

The second reason many companies outsource is because they need the expertise in order to move faster in marketing their products or services and to show better performance, and outsourcing allows them to acquire this expertise quickly through the vendor. This is true about outsourcing generally, especially about IS services that evolve and transform at such a rapid pace that it is hard to remain an expert on an IS topic without continuous training. Let us track the progress of IS technology and expertise topics from the 1960s when commercial computing began.[37] Beginning in the 1960s, almost every 5 years there has been a revolution in computing: machine code (think of code in hexadecimal digits), to assembly, to COBOL and FORTRAN, to structured programming and 3GL (third-generation programming languages), to application generators and 4GL (fourth-generation programming languages), to object orientation, to open source, and currently to mobile computing (running applications on smartphones) and Cloud computing. Together with this transition there has been a parallel advance in databases from flat files to indexed files and ISAM, to VSAM, to hierarchical databases such as IMS/DB and network ones such as IDMS, to relational databases starting with System R and going through DB2 and its competitors such as Oracle and SQL Server, to object-oriented databases. With each of these transitions there was a paradigm shift in how programming was done. Keeping up to date has required relearning a whole new philosophy almost every 5 years or so.

With such a rate of change, companies that are not IT companies have little choice but to rely on vendors to provide these services, especially considering their need to respond quickly when a new technology arrives so as to stay in the competition. Even IT companies often need to acquire expertise they do not have from other companies. In some cases it may be impractical to do otherwise. A company that needs to fine-tune its database regularly can do so with its own database administrator (DBA), but every now and then there will be a complicated problem that a regular DBA is not trained to solve. This would be the kind of problem that only an expert can solve. These experts are not readily available and are quite expensive, and they need to continually learn in order to keep up to date themselves with the technology. It makes no sense to hire one of these experts when the company only needs these services once in a blue moon. It is easier to outsource these database-tuning services to a vendor, especially as the expert tuning them can do so without being on-site. It also makes sense to outsource in this case only if the client knows what it wants and realizes what the risks are and what steps need to be taken to control these risks.

An Example of How Outsourcing Achieves Cost Cutting and Speed to Market

Suppose your company decides to develop its own customer relationship management (CRM) web-based system. You could develop it in-house, but that would take several months, if not years, and might require hiring many IT and IS experts, many of whom your company would not need full time once the project is completed. Alternatively, you could outsource the development of the system to IBM, Infosys (one of the largest Indian software outsourcing giants), or any of many other software vendors for a fraction of the cost of developing it in-house, have guaranteed quality and speed of delivery, avoid the mistakes first-timers make, and do all this without the need to establish a new IS department. Moreover, in contrast to developing in-house, if your company outsources then it knows exactly how much the project will cost and when it will be delivered. As long as the project is standard, meaning your CRM looks and behaves as all others do and has no special unique features to it except minor customizations, your company can also be reasonably assured that the CRM will work correctly from the day it is released, which is not always the case with custom-made software. It is a win-win situation.

The vendor can afford to be so much cheaper because it has the expertise your company lacks. And, having developed similar projects for many other clients, it has the economies of scale. Moreover, this being a software project it is quite possible that the vendor will reuse code. Reusing code it has already developed and tested in other projects should save the vendor the need to actually write a lot of the code it is charging the client for as well as allow it to reuse its expertise from previous projects. The result should be therefore faster, cheaper, and better work. The vendor has probably done so many equivalent projects in the past that it also knows how to manage such projects and to correctly estimate their complexity and development time. Outsourcing in such a case allows the client to control many of the development risks in the project.

It is because of such economies of scale and reuse of code and expertise that companies sometimes used to expect as much as 40% savings on their costs. Actually, factoring in that a programmer in India used to earn a tenth of what an American did, and that an Indian programmer on average is just as good, then, on the face of it, this does seem rather reasonable. This, of course, was too good to be true. There are always costs the client forgets to include, and the vendor forgets to mention. In the long term such savings are not realistic. In fact, many CIOs tell me that if a project is going to last more than several years, it may be cheaper to bring it back in-house, not to mention the crucial issue of better quality control in-house and the ability to implement changes faster.

Alliances

Other reasons companies outsource is because of the business benefits and connections it gives them. After all, at least partly, outsourcing is a strategic business question and not just a matter of operational considerations such as cost cutting and acquiring expertise.

On a company level there are additional reasons why companies outsource. A primary one is to gain access to markets. This is especially true in the pharmaceutical industry, which is why so many American pharmaceuticals have outsourced their manufacturing operations to Ireland. Outsourcing thus to Ireland opens the gates of the European Union to American pharmaceuticals, not to mention the much lower corporate tax rate at only 12.5% and a very industry friendly and supportive government where chief executive officers (CEOs) can talk directly to government ministers. This outsourcing to Ireland, by the way, is so large that, as one government official told us, 1 in 13 employees in Ireland in 2007 was employed in these outsourced pharmaceuticals and high-tech companies, making Ireland one of the major pharmaceutical centers in the world.

Taxes and other government policies, such as the 12.5% corporate tax in Ireland and less labor regulations, also play a role in the strategic decisions companies make to outsource. European companies that need to deal with sharp fluctuations in demand, for example, sometimes outsource their manufacturing, and this includes their services, out of Europe. After all, in countries like the United States and China labor laws allow companies to easily lay off employees. This is not the case in Europe. In Germany workers who are laid off because of mergers must get a 5-year salary severance pay.

Of course, companies also outsource to cut costs—but, as we shall learn, cutting costs alone is not always a good enough reason to outsource, especially as the outsourcing company is still legally responsible.

The User Imperative

Last, but not least, a reason often overlooked in the literature but often mentioned by CIOs[38] is that users today think they know what IS are all about and that they have the budget to buy IS through outsourcing, thereby circumventing the IT department and the CIO entirely. This *user imperative to outsource* is based on user expectations and is indeed a temptation to CIOs too for *instant gratification*. Users have become accustomed to an IT department that often misses delivery dates and is over budget. Outsourcing presents these users with the possibility to buy the IS services ready-made with a known price and delivery date, with guaranteed quality, and without waiting in line till the IT department can deal with their request. Users today know what they want, know they can demand it, and know they can often purchase it directly through outsourcing. This is a game changer, although users often realize after the fact that things are not as rosy as they had thought. These users, not being IT-trained clients, may not always fully understand the complexity of IS and so think that outsourcing can be the panacea to their slow and over-booked internal IS department. Sometimes they are right, but not always. Either way, the result is that the CIO has an unexpected outsourced IS package that may not necessarily comply with internal standards of inner connectivity to other IS or with security regulations.

An example of this can be found in a discussion at a CIO roundtable.[39]

A telling example of this was given to us by the CIO of a bank: "I think as we continue to see the workforce evolve and, especially in our organization, as we continue to see our users become more and more tech minded, they continue to come up with fabulous ideas on their own. I think the only way that I would be able to reduce the number of requests is by blocking access to Google through our Web filters, which at times I contemplate doing. . . . We were having discussions before this about the user community going out and finding a freeware solution, which is fabulous, and we've already signed the contract for this, and we want you to know how to implement it because as good security folks we don't let you touch our servers in production. But then we have to come back after the fact and say, you know, freeware doesn't really work in the enterprise. They're usually going to come back and nail us for some licensing fees."

Another illustration came from the CIO of a university who retold this story: "They . . . come to central IT and say, 'Can you do this?' 'Oh, sure, you're in my two-year project, and what's the business value, and show me the return on investment,' and I demand all this stuff. And they [say], 'I can buy this solution here for $3,000, and I don't have to show an ROI, and I don't have to prove all this stuff out, and I don't need you to do it.' 'And I've got the money in my budget.'"

Dispelling Misconceptions

In the United States outsourcing, and especially outsourcing offshore (called "offshoring"), is often equated with bad things. It is often linked in people's minds to the loss of jobs and American know-how, and a reduction in product and service quality. The recall of Chinese toys with lead paint in 2007 is a good example of this.[40] But outsourcing, and this includes offshoring, also has a positive side for the U.S. economy. Outsourcing provides companies with access to capabilities and knowledge they lack. It allows companies to buy and manufacture cheaper products and services. It is a leading reason for the spread of wealth and democracy in the world[41] and in making the world, in the words of Tom Freidman, a flat world where Mumbai and Boston are both equally only one click away.[42] In this flattening-of-the-world process the greatest beneficiary has been the United States. The Dow Jones jumped in this period from around 1,100 points in

1983 to over 10,000 in 2010, with a short period of being over 14,000 in October 2007.[43] During this period there has been a $10K increase in the net value of U.S. households.[44] In fact, as much as one should cry out for the loss of U.S. jobs, one should not forget that in the United States today about 5 million people work for companies that are stationed abroad, that is, are offshore to the United States. That is, according to some estimates, about 4% of the U.S. workforce, accounting for 10% of capital investment in the United States, 15% of R&D, and 20% of U.S. exports.[45] Moreover, even Chinese companies, known for their cheaper labor cost advantages, are beginning to offshore to the United States because of better utilities, cheaper land, and local government support.[46] Offshoring has made the United States the linchpin of international economic activity and has benefited the United States so much that it has been in a recession only 5% of the time since 1982.[47]

Why Not to Outsource

Well, if outsourcing is so good why are so many small companies reluctant to outsource? There are many reasons for that. A common thread through all these reasons is that *a company should not outsource if it does not know what it wants or how to do it.* Companies forced to outsource by their shareholders and boards who are eager for quick profit are major reasons for outsourcing failure. This is especially a pity because boards typically do not have time to study and decide on IT matters and leave such "low-level" decisions to the CIO,[48] although boards are more involved in IT decisions when the IT is part of an offensive, rather than defensive, strategy.[49] Dominguez[50] estimates that this may be so in as much as 20% of the cases. In this context it is necessary to understand that outsourcing is a business decision, and like many other critical business decisions, there are many stakeholders involved and these stakeholders often have very different and even conflicting critical success factors (CSFs)—the three or four really important things one should pay close attention to all the time to achieve success. This type of herd mentality to outsource because everyone else seems to be doing it is unadvisable in the best of times. Outsourcing might be the right way to go, but a company must know why it is doing so, how to do it, and verify its CSFs before it starts.

Putting Things Into a Historical Perspective

Information systems outsourcing in the United States started as early as 1949 when automatic data processing (ADP) started handling out-sourced payroll. By 2005, 95% of *Fortune* 1000 companies outsourced, albeit only very selectively.[51] Smaller companies are more reluctant to outsource. By some estimates only 19% of non-*Fortune* 1000 companies outsourced in 2005.[52] Judging from CIO roundtables I attend, the reluc-tance of smaller companies to outsource remains. In part this is because the promise of large savings through outsourcing has not always material-ized. Average cost savings through outsourcing may be altogether as low as 10%, but many companies actually see their costs increase as a result of outsourcing.[53] These numbers are not surprising. Software development, going back at least to the "software crisis" declared by NASA in 1966, has always been notorious for costing more than expected and missing deadlines.

The Outsourcing Mind-set

Know and Control the Risks

If one could sum up in one sentence what the key to successful outsourc-ing is, or indeed in management as a whole, then this would be it:

故曰：知彼知己，百戰不殆；不知彼而知己，一勝一負；
不知彼，不知己，每戰必殆

(No, this does not mean outsource to China or in Chinese—verb, noun, adjective, or adverb—is the answer.) These are the famous words of Sun Tsu in *The Art of War* presented in the quotation at the beginning of this chapter. As translated by Wikipedia this is what it says: "So it is said that if you know your enemies and know yourself, you can win a thousand battles without a single loss. If you only know yourself, but not your opponent, you may win or may lose. If you know neither yourself nor your enemy, you will always endanger yourself."[54] Put into perspec-tive, the vendor is not the enemy and should not be treated as such. Nev-ertheless, a company that does know its own risks and needs and does not know the risks and needs of the outsourcing vendor it is engaging with should not try to outsource. Only a company that understands itself and understands the vendor should engage in such an endeavor—and one might add here going beyond Sun Tsu that the outsourcing company should also understand the market terrain and the technology and its timing that are involved.

This is a critical point. Managing outsourcing is about understanding and managing the risks involved because outsourcing the IS of a company can be very risky. Indeed, outsourcing will magnify existing IS-related risks and introduce a host of other serious risks. *The key to successful outsourcing is recognizing these risks and controlling them or avoiding outsourcing altogether when they cannot be controlled.* The IS are figuratively speaking the equivalent of the nervous system of the company. IS outsourcing failures—be it bad contracting, overblown expectations, problematic transition, not meeting CSFs and milestones, missed schedules and budget targets, and so on—share the same problems: not knowing yourself, and not knowing the vendor, and not knowing the technology and market.

Risk management is the key. Indeed, as a senior manager in IBM once told me, the job of a manager is to control risks, and when this is not possible then at least to manage these risks to an acceptable level. Controlling risks means managing so there are no blips, no risks of mishaps. It is about making sure everything runs as it is supposed to and bringing variance acceptably close to zero so there are no surprises, no missed schedules, no overextended budgets, and no risks of things not being done when and how and at the level of quality they need to be done.

The Definition of Risk

Managers have responsibilities and their tasks, at the highest level of abstraction, is to make sure these responsibilities are carried out properly. To define what "carried out properly" actually means, each one of these tasks has, or should have, measureable CSFs. As Drucker put it, "If you can't measure it, you can't manage it."[55] Thus, for example, making sure that production rates, sales levels, service quality, product quality, response time, meeting schedules, having few glitches in newly implemented software, and so on—all these are examples of manager's responsibilities—are carried out correctly there should be a measure of what is expected and how to measure it. This level of what is expected should preferably be a number that can be unambiguously measured. The few really crucial aspects of these measured tasks are the CSFs.

Risk means an unacceptable deviation from the predefined accepted range of values of the CSF.

This definition of risk is why continuous measurement of important statistics is so crucial. Without measurement one cannot know if the CSFs have been met and if something that needs special attention to is happening. Meeting the scheduled milestones in a project is a good example of this. Being on time in a project is a CSF, especially true in the case of software development. That is why projects are broken into milestones and continuously monitored. The CSF here would be meeting the delivery date of each milestone, perhaps allowing or tolerating a deviation of a day or so in the interproject submilestones. Missing a deadline by more than this toleration rate is a risk that managers are employed to control for.

Safety Margins

Controlling risk is by no means an easy thing. It means first of all knowing what the real issues are, what they entail, how to measure them, what acceptable levels are, how to avoid them, how to manage them, and having the right mind-set to address them, although, figuratively, you never know what alligators there are in the water till you jump in. That is why part of managing risks, and this is especially true in outsourcing from both the client and the vendor sides, is to take a safety margin.

Safety margins are crucial because one never knows enough about what unexpected things, read this as risk, will pop up. When the negotiator in our company—a software vendor—asked for a time estimate on a software project, we as project managers would make our own estimate and then multiply it by 4 before giving the estimate to our negotiator—and we still had to struggle to meet schedule. The mind-set was a Murphy's Law: if anything can go wrong, it will.[56] The case of Boeing's Dreamliner 787 is a case to bear in mind.[57] Boeing is a very well managed company and has been outsourcing parts of its production for decades. When Boeing decided to manufacture its new 787 Dreamliner it decided to take advantage of its considerable expertise in outsourcing. This may have been a wise decision because of the enormous R&D and other costs involved, because it allowed Boeing to take advantage of the expertise other companies accumulated that it did not have, and because it allowed Boeing to forge international strategic alliances that could help it in marketing and with its competition with Airbus (some of the good reasons to outsource outlined earlier in this chapter)—but it also exposed Boeing to additional risks beyond its control. These risks eventually forced Boeing to delay entry of the new aircraft five times because the suppliers did not live up to what their contracts required. Eventually, Boeing purchased some of its suppliers so it could better control the manufacturing scheduling of these vendors.[58] Murphy's Law is alive and kicking.

In Lieu of a Boilerplate

Although there is no such thing as a boilerplate solution to outsourcing, there are some structured guidelines one can follow that summarize the material discussed in this chapter.

Step 1: Do Your Homework

It is a common theme in many testimonies about outsourcing that if you do not know what you are doing and what you expect as an outcome, then do not do it. This is akin to what Sun Tsu said. Here is a list of at least some of the key topics you must know. This is not intended as a comprehensive list but as a guide. You must do your homework before you decide whether and how to outsource. It might sound obvious that to just follow the bandwagon is unwise, but as we shall see in the next chapters that is precisely how certain parts of the market behave.

1. **Know your expected benefits.**
   - *Cost savings.* Most companies outsource because they expect cost savings. By some estimates this figure might be as high as 94%.[59] This is a good reason. The bottom line is always the bottom line

and should always be part of the considerations. However, make sure to calculate all the additional costs your company will incur. As some CIOs I talked to reminded me, the vendor may promise you a 40% savings on costs, but once you bring in the additional transaction and monitoring costs your company will incur once it switches to outsourcing then the number becomes more like 10%. Now, 10% is a formidable savings, but it is not as drastic as 40%, and once you bring in the additional nonfinancial costs and risks, it may not be worth it.

- *Your acquiring expertise.* As we shall discuss in chapter 5, as companies mature in their outsourcing philosophy the next stage after cost savings is acquiring expertise. This is a really good reason to outsource. If you cannot currently do it and the vendor can immediately and with expertise, then outsource. Hiring a top-notch DBA to fine-tune the databases in your company would be a primary example of outsourcing for this purpose. Again, this is not a panacea. As some CIOs remind me, if you plan to outsource to obtain a certain expertise and continue to do so for several years, then it might be cheaper to hire someone and do it in-house.

- *Forging strategic alliances.* In some cases companies outsource because they need a strategic partner. Many U.S. software companies and pharmaceuticals have either captive centers or joint ventures with Irish companies so they can enter the EU.

- *Time to market.* If the vendor can manufacture faster than your company can then in many cases this is a benefit worth considering.

- Realize the need to meet users' perceptions (and these may be exaggerated) of the possibility of achieving *instant gratification through outsourcing.*

2. **Know your costs.** As in other cases of cost-benefit analysis, you should know your costs. These might outweigh any benefits you hope to achieve.

- *Transaction costs.* Having another company do the work for you does not allow you to abdicate responsibility. Your company will incur many additional transaction costs (costs in managing this relationship). More on this in chapter 4.

- *Lack of control.* Apart from additional transaction costs there is another issue your company will need to contend with—lack of control. When a vendor does the work for you, you do not have as much control over the process, its quality, what subcontractors are hired, work conditions, and so on. But you are still responsible.

- *Being insulated from new technology.* In the high-tech world there is a revolution every 5 years and a new technology every 18 months or so. Outsourcing may insulate your company from recognizing these developments and realizing profit from them, and this may cause your company to be late to adopt new technology. After all, the vendor is in this for the money. Giving your company access to new technologies is something a vendor would consider, but mainly within the context of making more money. Your company, on the other hand, needs to know about these new technologies to stay ahead.

- *Adding distance from your clientele.* For-profit companies exist for the sole purpose of selling their goods and services to their customers. If by outsourcing your company adds another layer between itself and its paying customers, this will have consequences. When your company does not know what its clients need because it is further removed from them (because there is a vendor providing these goods and services) then your company may not be aware of new tastes and demands the clientele has.

3. **Understand the process.** While doing a cost-benefit analysis is something drilled into MBA students, there is also the need to understand the process of outsourcing. We shall discuss this throughout the book, but even at this stage remember that outsourcing is not a sign-and-forget process. Your company must remain involved throughout the process, even if it is outsourced.

   - *CSF.* Before you begin, define the critical success factors (CSFs), and make sure all the stakeholders are on board on this. CSFs should be measureable and there should be critical values assigned to each. These CSFs should be assigned at the overall contract or project level and at each milestone along the way.

   - *It is all about risk control.* The task of a manager is to control risks. The same applies here too. Here is a list of some of the recurring risks in IT outsourcing: Do you understand the requirements? Do you have the right person in control? Have you addressed the people issues (remember, IT projects may not succeed temporarily because of technology problems, but they will surely fail because of people problems, such as user resistance)? Do you understand the contracting process? How will you handle the adverse selection risks (identifying a trustworthy vendor) and the moral hazards (not knowing exactly what the vendor is really doing)?

- *And know how to measure these risks and what the acceptable levels of each are.*

CHAPTER 2

Review of Current IS Outsourcing Topology and Trends

Living is easy with eyes closed, misunderstanding all you see.
—John Lennon, The Beatles, "Strawberry Fields"

Overview of Topology

Outsourcing is letting out work, work a company may have done in-house, to another company that specializes in that type of work.[1] If done correctly, apart from cutting costs, this allows the client company to concentrate on its core activities and better define its competitive standing.[2] In this regard outsourcing somewhat parallels the traditional dichotomy in information systems (IS) strategy, that is, "make or buy." Many of the regular issues pushing one way or the other apply here, too: cost analysis, limited set of products or services, short- or long-term objectives, level of interdependence, and access to resources.[3] However, the nature of the project and the contracting that governs it are both quite different.

In industry interviews with chief information officers (CIOs) partly in preparation for writing this book the feedback was that only about a third of companies outsource their IS services, and these few are mostly the larger ones, and even they are very cautious about it. Most of the CIOs interviewed, including from small companies, were very selective about what they outsource and how they go about it. Their attitude is much in agreement with the risk control strategy advocated in chapter 1. When companies do outsource there is a clear preference for *fixed price* contracts over other types of contracting governance. In this chapter we shall review contract types and these current trends.

Governance

Governance is about how the contracting relationship is governed. It is about the type of contracts and the type of contractual controls put into place to reduce risks. Outsourcing contracts are usually fixed price contracts, some are **time and materials**, and a few are a combination of the two. Academic research examining a small number of vendors or clients have found the same preference,[4] as is the case in other industries, too.[5]

Fixed Price

Outsourcing work is typically let out on the basis of either fixed price or time and materials. The key to a fixed price contract is that the price, schedule, and deliverables are all defined in advance, at the time the contract is signed, and variation in any of these can result in a penalty. Accordingly, in a fixed price contract the vendor is given a detailed requirements document that binds both the client and the vendor to exactly what needs to be delivered, how, when, and at what quality, along with a detailed schedule. Typically, this requirements document is accompanied by a detailed service level agreement (SLA) and a detailed schedule of payment and delivery milestones. The payment and delivery milestones do not necessary fully overlap, as there may be several delivery milestones for each payment milestone. Once the contract is signed there are clear deliverable requirements on both the client side and the vendor side. On the client side these might include making key personnel and documentation available and answering queries adequately within a given timeframe. They might also include making resources and information available. On the vendor side these might include the software modules that are to be delivered and when, exactly what each module will do, what testing and other quality-control procedures will be followed, how the training of client personnel will be done, and the schedules of all of these. The contract may also include specific key personnel the vendor is obliged to have on the project and how many hours a week or a month they must spend on the project.

Fixed price contracts are especially suitable when the client knows exactly what it wants and can convey this exactly in the requirements specifications—thereby opening the tender to the market and letting vendors compete on price. A good example is a client that needs to install several hundred new PCs of a specific specification with specific software by a certain date at specific sites. The definitive characteristic of a fixed price contract is that the client defines exactly what is needed and the vendor develops it within the timeframe and quality assurance levels as specified in order to be paid upon delivery. It does not mean the client should abrogate control or inspection.

The great advantage of fixed price contracting from a client's point of view is that the client is supposedly in control of its costs, schedule, IS development, and IS risks—assuming the vendor can be trusted to deliver. If everything goes according to schedule, this type of contracting controls financial risks (in knowing exactly how much everything will cost and when payments are due) and operational risks (in the assurance that the IS project will be delivered on time and within quality specifications and will be deployed successfully). This is extremely important in the context of IS because IS have always suffered from what NASA called as early as 1968 the "software crisis": spending more than the allocated budget, missing the delivery dates, and having too many glitches.[6] Choosing to contract on a fixed price is therefore quite a temptation to non-IS managers who know little about the real complexity of IS, and who are irritated by the seeming incompetence of the IS team who often miss their schedule on deliverables, end up costing more than expected, and have glitches. To these managers outsourcing at a fixed price does seem to be a panacea—but the reality of how complex IS are is more daunting than many predict.[7]

One reason fixed price projects fail, and why therefore time and materials are preferred at least theoretically in some cases, is that the fixed price contract is an obligation to the client as well as the vendor. The client is expected to know exactly what is needed and to be able to describe it adequately with all the accompanying details this requires. This is not an easy feat. As we discussed in the previous chapter, software projects can be likened to jigsaw puzzles where you never know if a piece is missing or mis-cut until you put it all together. Going with a fixed price contract requires a lot of preparation because a project's requirements are almost always incomplete. This is because all the involved managers and client stakeholders could never read the thousands of pages of requirements and see all the inconsistencies and missing parts. If the requirements specifications are incomplete, the concrete obligation in the specifications to the vendor will come back to haunt the client, who then must pay for expensive changes (expensive because now the vendor has a lock-in on the client). This is a risk clients should not ignore when they consider fixed price contracting.

Put into perspective, things may not be as bleak as they look. Vendors want the project to succeed, too, and so often they take their own safety margins when pricing their bids so that they have enough wiggle room to add minor additions to the requirements or to make minor changes to the IS specifications without reopening or renegotiating the contract. That is why it is crucial to have an element of trust in the business relationship between the client and the vendor and not base the relationship entirely on the contract alone.

Shifting the Risks in Fixed Price Contracts

The main reason clients prefer fixed price contracts is that going with a fixed price contract shifts the financial, operational, and development risks to the vendor. Assuming the vendor does not mess up, this is a wise decision. If the vendor does mess up, however, the client too will have to pay for it. To avoid or at least reduce the risk of such outcomes, many CIOs in large companies, when interviewed for this book, said their policy is to contract only within a small select group of vendors they really trust and who realize the relationship is long term; other vendors are not even considered unless they have some unique skill that this small cadre of select vendors does not have. Being in this select group opens up business opportunities, and being excluded means forfeiting these opportunities, so the few select vendors have a very good reason to want the project to succeed. A vendor in this select group will accordingly invest over and above what the contract says because it knows that even if it were to lose on this contract the client will make it up later on. We saw the same pattern in a large European bank we studied.[8] The bank had a select number of vendors it worked with, limiting its contracts to this small cadre it really trusted. But even then, only those vendors with whom the bank had contracted extensively in the past were given the contracts that were more profitable and less risky in terms of vendor time and materials. That way the vendors had a lot to lose if they did not deliver and a lot to gain if they did.

Time and Materials

The advantage of a fixed price contract, then, is that both the client and the vendor know exactly what is required of them (or at least they think they do initially): deliverables, quality, price, and schedule. But fixed price contracts hold the risk that if the requirements are imperfect then it is a double-edged sword where these advantages become disadvantages. Requirements are not known in detail before the project begins. To deal with such cases clients and vendors turn to the time and materials type of contract.

The defining characteristic of time and materials contracts, also called "cost plus," is that the vendor is paid as a function of the time and materials it invests, which in IS projects usually means payment by billable hours. Paying by billable hours means that all engaged vendor employees are assigned an hourly fee based on their education and experience (e.g., experienced programmers in the United States may be paid in the range of $55 an hour, database administrators (DBAs) at a $62 hourly rate, and project managers $110 an hour).[9] This method of billing gives the vendor a fixed profit on each of its engaged employees with practically no financial risk as long as things run smoothly.

Time and materials contracting is not the same as hiring "heads" (i.e., paying the vendor for experts who work as temporary outside contractors and who do as the client instructs them, much as would a temporary employee, but who are paid their salary from the vendor; technically this is not outsourcing). Time and materials contracting is not an equivalent of temporary employees because in a time and materials contract the vendor still manages the project. It is the vendor, and not the client, who decides on internal scheduling and staffing. In time and materials contracting the client's requirements are not as concrete as they are in a fixed price contract, therefore the vendor is paid by time invested rather than by deliverables.

In a time and materials contract the financial, and in some cases the developmental risks as well, are shifted to the client. Financial risks are about the project costing more than budgeted. Developmental risks are about not being able to develop the IS that are supposed to be developed within time and quality requirements. Shifting these risks to the clients is necessary because in this type of governance the requirements are less specified upfront and can, and often will, change after the contract is signed. As a result, the overall price is unknown at contract signing, although the range of cost is usually predetermined. Thus, in a time and materials contract the vendor is obliged to deliver the IS to the satisfaction of the client, although at the onset the contract is relatively more vague on what exactly is required than is a fixed price contract.

On the face of it, time and materials should be the preferred mode of outsourcing for *both* clients and vendors. This, however, is not always the case. Fixed price contracting allows the client more financial control, which is critical because IS projects often overrun their budget as requirements escalate out of control.[10] The emphasis is on the bottom line, and fixed price contracting is therefore preferred as a way to control cost risks. This is because ultimately the person who signs the contract is the chief financial officer (CFO) or someone who answers to the CFO. The CFO is charged with reducing financial risks, and overrun costs are one of these financial risks. Moreover, allowing the vendor to bill the client on hours worked is practically like giving the vendor a blank check. That is precisely the kind of financial risk the CFO is there to control, so little wonder CFOs prefer fixed price projects. And so, although the IS operational risks (how the project is managed) and development risks (whether the IS will ultimately perform as expected and be delivered on time) are also crucial, they are of less importance because they are in the realm and risk of the IS project manager, and not the CFO. Again, it all boils down to controlling risks, except that each stakeholder sees and cares about different risks. The CFO cares about financial risks whereas the IS project manager cares about IS operational and development risks.

Vendors also prefer fixed price projects because there is more profit (although also more risk) for them in these projects.[11] Vendors know what their exact costing is (costing is the price, or cost, assigned to each aspect of a contract or project) while the client does not, and so the vendor can take advantage of this information asymmetry to charge higher prices. Indeed, fixed price contracts are often more profitable to IS vendors.[12] With fixed price contracts the vendor needs to report less frequently to the client than it does with time and materials contracts and so can cover up its own mistakes. Moreover, reporting only when required at each milestone, and even then reporting only on the outcomes (as is typical in fixed price contracts), allows the vendor to shift its own personnel among projects as needed, which is something the client normally would not be too happy to know about. Vendors do not like to work with the client breathing down their necks and limiting their ability to shift people among projects, and IS vendors are no exception.

Runaway Risks in Time and Materials Contracts

The main risk to the client with a time and materials contract is that of runaway projects. If the users on the client side are not forced to limit their requests (and this would require a project manager with a backbone who can stand up to powerful managers in the client's organization and refuse to let them add features once the requirements document has been closed), they will continually add features and make changes to the IS. Features may be added for a variety of reasons. This is not necessarily an indicator of something wrong with the software or the way the project is managed. On the contrary, continuous adaptation can also be a sign of good software. As users start using new IS they realize the new IS can solve other problems and improve other processes they did not initially think about.[13] While this is a good sign, it can also lead to uncontrolled project escalation and loss of financial control. Another reason for an escalation in the scope of the requirement is that some of the needed software modules may not have been initially approved by the client project management team in their attempt to cut costs. Projects typically cost more than initially expected, and they may have needed to cut features and modules out of the project in this way. Failure to keep a tight control on the requirements, much harder in times and materials contracts than in fixed price ones, can reintroduce such modules back into the project in an uncontrollable manner, leading to cost escalation and loss of financial control, and make it impossible to know how much the project will end up costing or when it will ultimately be delivered. This adds to the financial risk the client faces, which is why CFOs prefer not to contract on a time and materials basis. Of course, just because the contract is time and materials does not mean the users on the client side can add new features at will. The difference in this regard between a fixed price and a time and materials contract is that in a fixed price contract the client project manager must veto requests for additional features at the requirements phase of the project, while in the time and materials contract this veto must be yielded also during the development and implementation phases. Not having such a strong project manager in charge, especially in a time and materials project, can mean runaway projects and uncontrolled escalating costs.

Time and Materials With a Price Cap

One way of controlling these escalating costs in time and materials contracts is to set a price cap on the cost of the project. Again, it requires a strong project leader on the client side to be able to say no and veto additional requests. This is harder than it sounds because each additional request may be very small and its functionality may indeed be justified and yet, put together, these additions mount up and cost can easily escalate. This type of governance is rather rare in IS outsourcing.

X+Y Contracting

Another way of reconciling fixed price and time and materials contracting to gain the advantages of both is to have an X+Y contract. In an X+Y contract the initial development of the project, the X, is managed as a fixed price contract while the later additions, the Y, are typically managed by a time and materials contract. This allows the client to control costs and schedule on the major part of the project, the initial development, while maintaining the flexibility it will need later on to add additional features and enhancements to the IS as needed on a time and materials basis. Stating at the initial (and bigger) fixed price stage what key experts of the vendor it wants to have in the subsequent time and materials stage allows the client to lock in the key personnel of the vendor in the latter stage. Although statistics on how frequently this method is used are not available, working on the vendor side, I have seen this method used quite frequently among skilled large clients.

Accounting for missed features in the requirements in the X phase by having these features eventually added in the subsequent Y phase allows the client the safety margin it will almost certainly need. This point is more acute than one might expect. In many cases I have observed the IS management on the client side negotiate, and compromise, on the budget that would be devoted to the project. This negotiation happens both (a) internally with those who hold the purse on the client side and (b) in the case of large IS projects, after the tender has been published during negotiations with the vendors on the details of the price. At both stages the client's IS management needs to cut out features so the budget will suffice for the compromised cost of the project. Sometimes whole critical modules need to be cut out. This puts the client's IS management in a bind. On the one hand, the client cannot reopen the tender and add the features back in because the budget for doing so has not been approved. On the other hand, these features are necessary and need to be added. Applying the X+Y contracting method allows the client's IS management to reconcile this by bringing the crucial modules that were cut out back in to the project through the back door at the Y phase.

This keeps all the stakeholders happy, that is, controlling the risks they are charged with managing. Those in charge of the budget, the CFO and accounts payable, are happy because they control the big expense they need to control in the X phase with the initial big fixed price cost. The Y phase is typically much smaller, not large enough to be of major financial concern. The users are happy because the IS works as promised and no crucial modules are left out, even if these modules are delivered at the Y phase and not right at the beginning in the X phase. The vendor is happy because the Y component of the project is a risk-free time and materials contract and allows the vendor to reduce its developmental risks in the X phase. Any left-out module or missed specified feature in the X phase can be corrected or added into the project in the Y phase without reflecting negatively on the deliverables of the X phase. And the client's IS management is happy because it controlled its own development and vendor relationship risks successfully. Anything it may have done wrong or missed in the X phase can be conveniently corrected in the Y phase without reopening the contract.

Transaction-Based Governance Method

In the transaction-based governance method the client is charged by the number of transactions, sometimes with different tariffs depending on the range of the number of transactions processed. This is quite a bit like cell phone contracts where the client pays by air minutes used. Examples of this method include help desk and training. The method is more popular with information technology (IT) outsourcing where the client may be billed monthly by CPU usage or by the amount of memory used.

Cloud Computing

Another option for outsourcing is to rely at least partially on Cloud computing. Thus, instead of custom-designed IS or services made to specifications either in-house or through traditional outsourcing, a client can opt for a standardized service provided by the vendor at the vendor site. Gmail, discussed in the previous chapter, is a primary example of this. Rather than maintain an internal e-mail service or outsource the maintenance of such a service, a company can rely on standardized, and in this case mostly free, services without having anything to do with the management or oversight of the service.

Although some of the concepts of Cloud computing have been around at least since Google unveiled Gmail on April 1, 2004, its definition is still evolving. As the U.S. National Institute of Standards and Technology (NIST)[14] defines it, there are five characteristics of Cloud computing. These are on-demand self-service, broad network access, resource pooling, rapid elasticity, and measured service.[15] The cost savings here can be dramatic. Salespersons I spoke to from companies such as Agilysys[16] claimed they could cut storage and data management costs by as much as 20% by moving their clients to a Cloud environment and do so without compromising the security of the data. Such savings can be achieved by taking advantage of economies of scale in large **server farms**.[17]

On-demand self-service means that no matter what services and computing capabilities the client needs they are automatically made available without the need of human interaction with the service provider. And so, for example, if a client needs more disk storage capacity or more computing power from Amazon.com or Microsoft, it is only a click away. And this click is done over the network with standard mechanisms on a thin client platform, such as smartphones, personal digital assistants (PDAs), and laptops showing *broad network access*, that is, the ability to connect through the Internet using a wide variety of technologies. The provider can provide these services on demand because it applies *resource pooling*, which means the computing resources are pooled so the provider may use the same resources to provide service to many clients, shifting resources among these many clients as their demands change. In doing so the provider can respond rapidly to changes in service demands by the clients who might need to rapidly scale up or scale down the services they are buying. It would indeed seem to the clients that the resources are unlimited. This ability to seem to the client as though the provider resources can be added or removed in an instant is called *rapid elasticity*. And, finally, these services are a *measured service* so the provider automatically measures and monitors the activities to provide a transparent service.

All these amount to making Cloud computing resources available in much the same way as buying electricity or cell phone service from a utility. It is there when you need it, wherever you are, providing as much of the service as needed by pooling the resources across customers, and providing any amount required immediately, while billing for the exact services provided. Moreover, behind the scenes these services are being continually fine-tuned so that they can be produced and maintained in an optimal manner—just as an electric service utility does. Even companies well entrenched in the more traditional client-to-vendor computing relationships, such as SAP, are planning to provide such services.[18]

The NIST[19] classifies Cloud computing into three service models: SaaS, PaaS, and IaaS. *Cloud software as a service* (SaaS) enables the client to activate the application through a thin client such as a website or a cell phone but have it actually run on the provider's infrastructure. Gmail and other types of web-based e-mail are primary examples of SaaS. Other cases of SaaS include supervisory control and data acquisition (SCADA) systems. SCADA are systems such as those that allow remote control of dams, grids, and factories through the Internet. *Cloud platform as a service* (PaaS) is the ability granted to customers to run their own developed or bought Cloud applications on the Cloud oblivious of the infrastructure of servers, operating systems, networks, and storage these require. Running apps on an iPhone falls into this category. Dedicated development environments that enable companies to develop such apps include Amazon Elastic Compute Cloud released in 2006 and Microsoft Azure released in 2010. *Cloud infrastructure as a service* (IaaS) allows the customer to run its own operating systems and control some other fundamental computing resources on the hosting cloud.

The cost savings incentives to move to SaaS can be compelling. Already, GSK, Coca-Cola, Enterprise, and others have moved to SaaS e-mail as a way of both cutting costs and allowing more of their employees access to their corporate e-mail network. The ready availability of these e-mail systems and their streamlined connectivity to other applications—such as enterprise resource planning (ERP), customer relationship management (CRM), and accounting—make this transition even more compelling.[20] Indeed, supporting the Cloud has become a major business initiative at Microsoft, joining other lead players such as Oracle, Google, and Salesforce.com.[21]

Needless to say, Cloud computing has its problems and should not be treated as a panacea. Some of the commonly made complaints against it, according to industry sources,[22] relate precisely to its supposed advantages: it is not infinite, it is too slow, it is not cheaper than going in-house, whether security is as good as when things are kept in-house is questioned, there are not enough standards to guarantee quality yet, and IT personnel fear losing their jobs. These problems are typical of a new IT technology, but they may make it just that much harder for CIOs to accept Cloud computing, as indeed some of them told us.[23] Industry sources[24] also identify complaints that relate to the flip side of the coin, the supposed advantages of outsourcing: that the client does not have enough control over process and resources; and buying services on the cloud may result in a lock-in by the vendor because the current lack of industry standards makes switching from one vendor to another difficult. Related to this, dealing with IT in mergers and acquisitions is so much harder when a Cloud vendor is also part of the story and when the IT manager at the client company does not have full control over what is happening. As to return on investment (ROI), industry reports argue that 32% of business technology professionals they surveyed think the ROI on Cloud computing is such that it will take between 1 and 2 years, and another 46% think it will take 3 to 5 years to recoup their investment.[25] Perhaps tellingly, in Carr's view at any rate,[26] those surveyed thought that Cloud computing will probably be used for commodity applications.[27]

Example

Suppose a bank needs to develop and implement changes in the way it manages its collateralized debt obligations (CDO) based on new regulations from the Federal Reserve and the European Central Bank. This is a multi-tier project. First, changes must be done to the current software modules so they will adhere to the new requirements, and this must be done in an impeccable manner and on time. The requirements as specified by the agencies are crystal clear, and conveniently there are several large vendors the bank trusts and has given out such work to in the past. This type of work might be best outsourced in a fixed price manner. This controls the financial risk and to some extent the developmental risks, too. Then, second, there is the matter of studying how the bank might utilize these changes to achieve a strategic advantage in the marketplace, such as by installing new trading mechanisms other banks may not yet have and that are not currently regulated. This may be an open-ended project, its requirements are not as detailed, and there are no ready-made packages that might support it. This type of project might be outsourced as a time and materials project, but, to control costs, it may have a maximum fixed price cap. Based on this second tier, a third tier might be implemented in which the proposed system in the second tier is developed. This might be done on an X+Y basis: X for the initial development and Y for the subsequent tweaking to improve it. This way the bulk of the financial risk, representing the bulk of the overall cost, is controlled for in the fixed price part, but there is enough leeway in the time and materials phase to correct for any mistakes. Of course, such new IS will require training, and considering that it is unclear how much training is needed, this could be transaction based: the vendor is paid a fixed amount for each hour-long training session of 20 employees.

Cloud computing as SaaS for the software module, as SAP is thinking of doing for some of its other modules,[28] might be relevant in tier 1 if the changes are standardized and regulated by the central banks and if they are guaranteed by the vendor to work correctly as ERP systems usually are. Cloud computing for storing the data as IaaS, however, would not be such an inviting option because of the sensitivity of the banking data.

Ownership

Ownership by the Client

A key question when outsourcing is who owns the software and intellectual property (IP) when the project is done. Typically, when a company contracts with a vendor to develop new IS or maintain an existing one, the client retains ownership on the IS. This is the traditional way IS outsourcing used to be done. Many of the CIOs interviewed for this book still use this model and in doing so treat the process of IS outsourcing as an exercise of doing more IS with less personnel. Outsourcing in this mode is either a way to free IS employees from their current maintenance jobs (which are passed to the vendor) so that they can develop new systems for the organization or a way to quickly and at less cost bring in expertise the client does not have but the vendor does. Outsourcing serves in part as a way to overcome the cost constraints put on the IT department but still leave the IT department in charge.

When the IS being outsourced are to be owned by the client it is often developed as a *turnkey* project, which means the project is delivered in fully operational fashion to the client. Think of it as buying a car. You enter it, turn the key, and drive away. In such projects the client is not heavily involved in the development of the IS. It still remains a key issue, however, who actually owns the IS. The vendor might want to keep a hold on it to ensure a lock-in of the client. The client, if it is capable, should want to own the IS itself precisely to avoid such lock-in and the cost advantages it gives the vendor. A variant on the turnkey concept is the *build-operate-transfer* mode. In this method of outsourcing, used often when the client is outsourcing offshore, the client contracts with an offshore provider to build the offshore center and then when it is up and running the client takes it over.

Ownership by the Vendor

In today's market quite often outsourcing is done as a way of relinquishing responsibility and passing it over to the vendor, especially with the advent of Cloud computing, although to give credit where it is due this was going on before the term "Cloud computing" was invented. When it concerns standardized operations, such as when a company decides to outsource its e-mail to Gmail or file income tax returns through Tur-boTax, things are relatively simple in this mode of outsourcing through Cloud computing. The client does not own the software or indeed the data residing on the server, but this is okay because there are regulations in place to protect privacy.

Even concerning more complex systems, such as airline reservation IS services, it makes sense to rely on an outsourcing vendor, although the risks in this case are higher. A case in mind is El Al, the Israeli air-line, who outsourced its online ticketing system to Lufthansa using the Amadeus system as part of the Star Alliance.[29] Online ticketing systems are critical for an airline because the profit of an airline carrier depends on the percentage of filled seats on each flight. Managing this process is complex and requires highly skilled IS personnel, although this type of IS is relatively standard and what suits one carrier probably suits the others, too. Viewing this situation, El Al decided to outsource the whole service to Lufthansa rather than continue maintaining such an expensive system in-house. There is really no IS risk involved for El Al. If the IS were to run into any problems he could be assured that Luf-thansa would immediately attend to it because its own survival depends on the same IS. Considering there was less IS risk in outsourcing this IS than in keeping it in-house, and considering it was cheaper to out-source, the decision was obvious. Moreover, although outsourcing this critical operational IS held the risk that Lufthansa could theoretically take advantage of the dependence of El Al on it, and although out-sourcing did mean the IS risk of losing the expertise involved, the deci-sion was made to outsource.

In this decision, EL AI, maybe unwittingly, followed the advice of Carr,[30] which we shall discuss extensively in chapter 3, to out-source standardized IS even if they are mission critical, because when all is said and done these systems are not that different from utili-ties such as electricity. A company may totally depend upon these IS, as it does with electricity supply, but there is no reason not to outsource it considering it is totally standardized and quality assured. Only mission-critical operations and hospitals have backup electric-ity manufacturing capacity; everybody else depends on the utilities to supply it. Outsourcing IS and IS operations in this way in the airline industry has been around for quite some time. Qantas, the Australian airline, has been outsourcing its IS to IBM since 2004 and to Telstra even before that as a way of moving away from direct IS management and cutting the costs of its IS.[31]

IS ownership becomes a critical question when it concerns unique new technology. The story of Intel and its invention of the microprocessor market, as presented by Christensen,[32] is a model case of this. Intel was contracted by a Japanese company to develop a chip for a pocket calculator. While developing this chip, the forerunner of the microprocessor running on all PCs, Intel scientists realized they had a marvelous invention on hand, and so they bought back the patent on this chip. The rest is history. Intel, a minor player in the computer chip memory industry, became the major player in the microprocessor market. Outsourcing that involves losing IP is a major risk.

Joint Ventures

To overcome this type of risk, as well as to overcome the cost of development, many companies outsource on a joint venture basis. This type of venture is more popular in the pharmaceutical industry than in IS, probably because it is more appropriate when all parties have IP involved and need to pool their IP together to make the new product. In this type of venture both, or more than two, companies jointly invest in the creation of a new company that, jointly owned by them, will develop the system or product.

An example of such a case is the recent joint venture between Élan, an Irish pharmaceutical with a new promising possible Alzheimer's drug, and the New Jersey–based giant Johnson & Johnson. Élan had run into cash flow problems, and Johnson & Johnson had the cash on hand and the spare manufacturing capability, so the two companies created a new joint venture to continue testing and then hopefully manufacture the drug. We shall discuss more of this joint venture in the upcoming chapters, but suffice it to say now that the CFO of Élan emphasized to us that it was not only about money and saving costs. It was about acquiring capabilities and about the ability of the two companies and their scientists to work together.[33] In our terminology, it was about controlling risks, and it is also about trust.

Location

Offshoring

When an outsourcing contract is given to a company located abroad it is called offshore outsourcing, or, in short, offshoring. There are many reasons why companies outsource abroad, rather than locally. Most often it is a matter of taking advantage of lower labor costs[34] combined with the ready availability in other countries of excellent engineers with very good English.[35] When outsourcing IS services began this savings amounted to quite a lot of money. U.S. programmers cost more than $90K a year while those in India cost at the time about $12K to $15K. Over the years these numbers started to equalize a bit. Experienced programmers and project leaders in top Indian companies today are already earning between 300,000 and 1,000,000 INR (1,000 Indian Rupees is about US$22).[36] Salaries in Israel and Ireland, the other two 3I countries (India, Israel, and Ireland) that are the destination of much of the U.S. offshoring activity, are much higher. The cheaper labor costs in India, however, come with the added risk of high employee turnover and the added risks resulting from there not being the same level of credit reports and criminal search databases as there are in the West.[37] A recent ACM (Association for Computing Machinery) report claims that many clients who offshore are not aware of these extra risks.[38] In recent years the Chinese software industry, always closely tied to the Chinese government, has begun to focus on being the target of offshored IS services.[39] This focus is currently more on the Japanese market than on the American one.

Nearshoring

A variant of offshoring is nearshoring. This term is used primarily for U.S. companies offshoring to Mexico and Canada, and Western Europeans companies to Eastern Europe. This reduces the cultural and distance-related risks and in the case of American companies provides preferred trading conditions under the North American Free Trade Agreement (NAFTA).[40]

Internal Outsourcing

Another variant on offshoring is outsourcing to a subdivision of the same company but in another country. This allows the client to take advantage of cheaper labor costs but at the same time reduce the risk of lack of loyalty and different legal codes and business cultures. This is very popular with many leading IS companies, including Intel, SAP, Microsoft, and IBM.[41] In discussions with CIOs in preparation for this book I was told that large non-IS companies also take advantage of such methods. The advantages are obvious. These companies retain control of the process and personnel involved on the vendor side, thus reducing many of the risks we have discussed and more we shall discuss, but at the same time taking advantage of the cheaper labor in other countries. This method also holds the advantage of allowing the client to pull key personnel from the vendor side to the client side, and vice versa, to facilitate the transfer of ideas and knowledge. It also allows companies to take advantage of programs governments in the 3I countries have to encourage high-tech companies to open shop there.

Internal outsourcing also reduces the risks associated with *loyalty*. Companies that outsource, thinking only of saving costs, often overlook the tremendous value the loyalty of their own employees brings them. Employees are naturally motivated in their own self-interest, which in practical terms means they will do what is needed within moral limits to retain their jobs and create chances for their own promotion. When employees work for their company, they have a vested self-interest in its success and in cases of renowned companies might even identify themselves at least partly with that company. As such these employees will stay and work overtime when necessary and will suggest ways to improve current processes. They will work more than just "by the book." That attitude of loyalty is considered by some authors to be the strength of German economy.[42] When employees are willing to go out of their way to support their company and take the initiative when necessary it creates an incomparable asset. Companies lose that when they outsource, because the loyalty of the workforce, if it exists, is to its employer: the vendor. These employees owe their employment to the vendor, and any promotion will come through the vendor.

Internal outsourcing overcomes this to a large extent because the vendor employees actually still work for the client and so their promotion and work security depend on the client and not only on the vendor. The story of Intel outsourcing its R&D to its Israeli subsidiary is a textbook case of how this method works to the advantage of all parties involved.[43] The Israeli engineers took the success of Intel Israel as a matter of personal pride and treated its success as their own. Even when the First Gulf War broke in 1991—when the United States invaded Kuwait in order to throw Iraq out and Iraq responded with Scud missiles against Israel— these employees came to work and made it a point of personal pride to deliver even before the date called for in the schedule. This loyalty convinced Intel to move more of its R&D and production to Israel, to the benefit of all involved.[44] You may hope that your own employees may behave this way, but it would be ridiculous to expect the employees of your vendor to do so. Companies that outsource to cut costs alone can only dream of such loyalty.

We shall discuss more on this issue in the context of agency theory in chapter 4.

Number of Vendors

Single and Multiple Sourcing

Another key consideration in managing the governance of outsourcing is the number of vendors. Again, the key questions here are what are the relative risks and their levels and how does one choose the combination of least risk. Outsourcing can be done to a single vendor. This is known as *single sourcing*. This vendor may choose to have subcontractors, in which case it is called *multiple integrated*. In a multiple integrated contract there is one vendor, the integrator, who is in charge. The outsourcing contract can prohibit the vendor from having any subcontractors or can explicitly say who those subcontractors are and what they are allowed to do. In the case of sensitive information it is often the policy that no subcontracting is allowed except in special circumstances and even then only with the consent of the client. This is necessary because while multiple integrated may reduce technical and developmental risks by allowing the primary vendor to subcontract part of the process to specialized experts, it also introduces additional risks concerning security and IP as well as coordination risks.

Alternatively, IS outsourcing projects may involve many vendors concurrently without any one of them being the lead vendor. This is known as *multiple sourcing*. The advantage of having many vendors is that the client can pick and choose the best one for each specific task and cut costs by having the bidding take place on smaller units of work. The risk in multiple sourcing is that the client cannot take advantage of there being a single vendor in charge, and so it is harder for the client to manage the process. Coordination can become quite an issue when things actually go wrong and there is a need to decide why things are not fitting together as they should. Unless the client is well versed in managing projects with many vendors, this could be a considerable liability. Coordination in this case is harder than it sounds also because each vendor does not want to be seen as the one who made the mistake or as the one who blames the client for making the mistake. Coordination among many vendors is, as in many other cases with software project management, often a matter of people issues more than technology issues.

Microsourcing

A variant on multiple sourcing is *microsourcing*. Microsourcing is a term coined by Carmel[45] to describe cases when an IS project is broken into many very small parts and each part is outsourced separately on the Internet through companies such as RentACoder.com. In contrast to multiple sourcing, where a large project is broken into smaller projects managed by many programmers each, in microsourcing the units of delivery are much smaller modules that are orders of magnitude smaller: A typical project on sites such as RentACoder.com costs in the $100 range, whereas a typical outsourcing contract—such as the one presented in Gefen and colleagues[46]—is in the range of $270,000. The advantage of microsourcing is that it takes the advantages of multiple sourcing to an extreme, allowing the client to break the IS project down into units of single functions. The risks are that it also takes the disadvantages of multiple sourcing to an extreme, making coordination a real problem.

Breaking up the project into such microcomponents has another advantage: nobody but the client sees the forest for the trees. In microsourcing the project is broken into such small pieces and distributed among so many vendors that it becomes very hard for any one of these vendors to see the whole picture and thereby endanger the IP of the client. This is in contrast to a typical outsourcing project where the vendor can, and indeed should, see the whole picture, and where therefore there is an IP risk.

It is common practice in many companies, including the large European bank discussed in Gefen and colleagues,[47] to split large outsourced IS projects into many smaller ones. Doing so allows the bank an increased measure of control over what the vendor is doing and the quality of its work. It also creates a strong incentive for the vendor to work hard and exceed expectations, knowing it stands a better chance of being considered for the next phase of the project only if it delivers as expected in the current phase. Discussions with bank managers revealed that the key issue here was again controlling risks.

Governance Types and Degree of Integration

The various options clients have in managing their IS outsourcing can be thought of as a continuum that starts with internal solutions (i.e., developing and maintaining the IS in-house) and moves all the way to totally relying on a market-oriented solution (i.e., Cloud computing). This can also be thought of as a move from in-house development (where there is a high degree of internal control over the process) through a series of increasingly market-oriented solutions (beginning with internal outsourcing to other locations within the same company but offshore) to a captive center in another country (owned by the client but not an integral part of it), to a joint venture with another company, to straightforward outsourcing through time and materials or fixed price, and finally to Cloud computing (where a standardized hosted IS solution is bought from the vendor). As a company moves along this line it loses more control over the IS and its development process but potentially gains more advantages in cost cutting and possibly in acquiring expertise quickly.

Degree of Outsourcing

The literature in the 1990s and early 2000s discussed the distinction between *total outsourcing* and *selective outsourcing* In total outsourcing more than 70% of the IS budget is outsourced. Some companies still do so. Qantas, discussed earlier, apparently chose this option when it signed an outsourcing contract worth AU$750 million with Telstra in 2004 to manage all of the voice, desktop, and network services—and showing the risks involved, this contract was "axed" several years later.[48] In all, by outsourcing, Qantas cut its IS workforce from around 1,400 in 1997 to only 375 by 2009.[49] The *total outsourcing* option has been extensively criticized over the years because of the lack of client control it entails. Indeed, a theme that comes up in every CIO roundtable I attend is the reluctance to even consider total outsourcing nowadays. *Selective outsourcing* is the alternative to outsourcing. In this option each IS project is considered on its own merit, whether or not it should be outsourced and how or if it should be retained in-house.

Another distinction made in the industry is between IS outsourcing (ISO) and business process outsourcing (BPO). In ISO the IS alone is outsourced. This may include the development of the IS, the data centers, networking management, help desk, recovery, and so on, but not the actual work done with the IS. In BPO, however, the business processes performed by the outsourced IS are also outsourced. In addition, outsourcing the activities the IS support might also include non-IS aspects, such as dealing with customers and managing finance. Obviously, the risks in BPO are higher. An excellent discussion on the distinction between ISO and BPO is available in Beulen and colleagues.[50]

Governance Example

This example is based, although modified, on the case of the European bank described in Gefen and colleagues.[51] As a matter of policy the bank prefers fixed price contracts and will give time and materials contracts only in very special cases where the nature of the project justifies it. Sixty-nine percent of the outsourcing contracts were fixed price, 23% were time and materials, and 8% were time and materials with a fixed cap contract. This is common in the industry. When the bank does give out time and materials contracts, and only as required based on the characteristics of the project, it usually does so to those very few select vendors with whom it has had many previous contracts. All the software is owned by the bank.

In addition to these outsourcing operations, the bank also employs additional staff that it hires from vendors and placement agencies on an hourly basis in lieu of hiring them full time. These employees are not treated as an outsourcing vendor's employees would be.

The process of outsourcing IS projects begins with a detailed requirements analysis. Based on this the tender is prepared with its detailed specification document and SLA. When the tender is ready, it is given to a limited number of trusted vendors the bank is willing to work with. All these vendors are there for the long run and are hired for their expertise. It would seem, based on the contract data, that bidding cost is not the primary reason a vendor is chosen. Rather, it is a matter of the vendor being trusted based on a long joint work record with the bank that really counts. Unless there are special circumstances, such as unique capabilities and skills, other vendors are not considered. This is not something unique to the bank but is common practice in the industry.

Controlling risk by choosing only vendors they trust is the name of the game. Indeed, if you think of it from the CIO's or IS project manager's perspective, it makes perfectly good sense. The risk the IS project manager is most concerned about is not the risk of paying a few percentage points higher than the cheapest bid. Certainly, it would be nice to save the company a few bucks, but that is not the critical success factor (CSF) of an IS project manager. Saving those few percents on the cost is the risk control of the CFO. The risks the IS project manager is most concerned about are whether the outsourced IS project will be developed correctly, deployed correctly, work correctly, have all the features it needs, and be on time. Saving a few bucks in the process is really a small issue.

In many cases, as is common with many experienced clients, the IS project managers in charge of the outsourced IS project estimate the cost of the project before they issue the tender, and then discard all those bids that are not close to the range they estimated. This is part of their risk control process. Bids that are too low may signify that the vendor either misunderstood the requirements or is *lowballing*. (Lowballing means bidding at a price that is below a reasonable profit or even below costs.) This is not out of any altruistic concerns. This is plain good policy. IS project managers eliminate bids that are too low because they want to make sure the vendor does not lose money on the project. Vendors who are about to lose money will cut corners in the way they develop the software, with the inevitable results of increased development and operational risks to the client. Remember, *the cost of a mistake in the software is not measured in the time it takes to correct it but in the damage it causes*, and this damage may be way beyond the cost of the entire project.

That price is not a primary consideration in the case of the bank is really not that amazing. The cost of failure in terms of missed European Central Bank deadlines and missed business opportunities is so high as to make saving a few percentage points on a contract a minor issue. Indeed, also in other markets for much smaller outsourced IS projects cost is not the reason developers are chosen.[52] So, making sure the vendor does not lose money is a way the client can reduce its own risks, or at least not introduce additional ones into the outsourced project. Of course, the client should not be a sucker in the process either and overpay. Rather, the contract should also be managed by the client, so it is in the vendor's own best interest to make it a success. Giving the project to a lowballing vendor also means running the additional risk of having the IS project manager lose credibility in the eyes of the CFO as to his or her ability to estimate costs. This may result in more difficulty in securing budget for future projects because the CFO may query whether the IS project management is inflating its cost estimates in these projects also.

When many of the bids are not within the expected range of costs, it is common to contact some of the vendors and ask them for their reasons for the costing they made, that is, how they reached the line by line cost of each element in the tender. This may result in recalibrating the expected cost, and securing more budget as necessary from the CFO, or withdrawing the tender.

Then, with this small number of remaining bids, all more or less within the same range and corresponding to the initial cost estimate the IS project manager made when requesting the budget for this project from the CFO, the client's IS project team chooses one of the vendors based on the expertise and qualification of the personnel the vendor is proposing to have on the project. This type of choice strategy, by the way, is not unique to the bank. It is common among many CIOs interviewed for this book. It is intended to reduce operational and developmental risks and avoid vendors who are there for quick profit. At this stage in the choice process, having a lower-priced bid is not the only consideration, because no two bids are the same, if only because of the different expertise of the key personnel each vendor is proposing. It may well be that a more expensively priced bid is actually a better bid considering the personnel. Contrary to common belief, when offshore vendors are given a contract it is not significantly cheaper compared to equivalent contracts given to local vendors. Based on our interviews with some of the people involved, this seems to be because of an implicit preference for local vendors. Choosing such vendors reduces cultural misunderstandings but also assures a more closely knit group of client and vendors, another method to reduce risks.[53]

It is all about controlling risk, even if the bank does not explicitly quote Sun Tsu.

In Lieu of a Boilerplate

In continuation of the structured guidelines in the previous chapter, here are more steps to follow as discussed in this chapter.

Step 2: Know the Landscape

There are many ways to outsource. It is imperative to know why you choose one way rather than another.

1. **Know your topography.**
   - Decide on your locus of control. Know if and why you want the contract to be fixed price, time and materials, or transaction based, or if you would rather have Cloud computing, a joint venture, a captive center, or internal outsourcing—and be aware of the risks.
   - Have detailed SLAs, and make sure to have reasonable safety margins. Scheduling is important. Gantt or Pert diagrams are excellent tools for mapping this scheduling. But whatever tool you choose, know when each milestone or other important event in the project is due.

- It is important to know where the bottom line is. It is important to consider whether to go offshoring, nearshoring, or onshoring.

2. It is also necessary to decide whether this will be a single sourcing, multiple sourcing, or microsourcing contract and whether it will be selective or total outsourcing.

3. **Have an exit plan.** Outsourcing can be, and often is, a major project. Before you embark on such a project, make sure to have an exit plan. You should know what the next step will be and, most importantly, there must be a contingency plan. Things will go wrong. Software projects are seldom, if ever, a success the first time around. Chances are the same will apply to your contract, too.

CHAPTER 3

The Technology Imperative

"Well, in our country," said Alice, still panting a little, "you'd generally get to somewhere else—if you run very fast for a long time, as we've been doing."

"A slow sort of country!" said the Queen. "Now, here, you see, it takes all the running you can do, to keep in the same place. If you want to get somewhere else, you must run at least twice as fast as that!"

—Lewis Carroll, *Through the Looking-Glass and What Alice Found There*[1]

Introduction

Going back to the discussion I had with the chief information officer (CIO) of a large Detroit automotive second-tier supplier in the prologue, perhaps the biggest mistake in outsourcing information technology (IT) is that of not understanding what the maturity level of the technology means. Indicative of this misunderstanding are his own words that he outsources IT all the time. There was nothing about risk mapping and control and not a word about measurement—always a big mistake. There was also not a word about different strategies depending on the type of IT, the vendor, or how the IT was used. And this is the crux of the matter: *Treating IT contracting as if it all belongs to one unified term of information systems (IS) outsourcing is wrong.* Organizations should differentiate between outsourcing standardized technology services, which is akin to what outsourcing is in other industries, and outsourcing the kind of IT that gives the organization a strategic advantage where the market is not yet set. We shall call the former the late majority segment of the market and the latter the early adopter segment of the market. The two are not the same and should not be confused. This chapter discusses this topic and the technological imperative created by the quick advent of technology.

To put things into perspective, in an excellent preview of outsourcing, Ashley[2] discusses questions one should ask before deciding to outsource. These questions involve knowing your expected costs and benefits, knowing the outsourcing process, and knowing the impact of outsourcing on your organization. Do you really know how your organization operates, and do you know your economics for outsourcing and how your company can manage layoffs? And then there is the always-pertinent issue of choosing the right person and deciding what to do next. These issues can be summarized, as they were in chapters 1 and 2, as knowing and controlling your risks. There is, however, another kind of risk that CIOs I talk to, including the CIO from Detroit, often miss in their calculations, and that is the issue of the technology itself. This chapter deals with this aspect.

Figure 3.1 shows the three interlocking circles one needs to understand in order to outsource knowingly. chapters 1 and 2 and this chapter are all in Circle 1. This is the basis of outsourcing. You must correctly address this circle before going on to the other two.

In discussing the technology imperative we shall introduce in this chapter two related imperatives and how each relates to outsourcing:

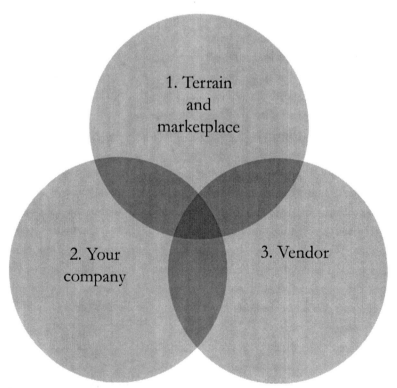

Figure 3.1. The three circles of outsourcing risks.

1. Market segmentation and with it the move toward standardization in a technology that goes through frequent revolutions and how this creates a technology imperative to outsource as well as the standardization conditions that support it.
2. The life cycle of technology in view of the diffusion of innovation theory[3] and the transition of IT toward being more like a utility and less like a custom-built system.[4]

Part 1: Market Segmentation

Looking back at the IT and IS market in the 1960s through the 1980s, one can see several big companies, IBM being the largest, providing products and services to the entire spectrum of IT and IS needs. This was accomplished through *proprietary technology*, which **locked in** the client so it could not easily switch to another provider. A client could go with IBM, Digital, Burroughs, Honeywell, or another company, each providing cradle-to-grave, proprietary, and noninterchangeable hardware, operating systems, and the software that runs on them. It used to be that if a company bought an IBM mainframe, then all the hardware, operating systems, databases, telecommunications, and even programming languages were all IBM. The same applied to other leading hardware and software providers. As a software engineer you knew IBM, or you knew Digital, or you knew Burroughs, and so on, but your detailed knowledge of how to do things, with some notable exceptions, did not cross over to the hardware and software of the other providers. There were some exceptions, mainly in the case of languages such as COBOL that were sponsored by the United States Department of Defense.[5] But, mainly, if you were trained on the machines of one company then you stuck to that one company.

Over the years this marketplace structure has changed dramatically. Instead of the silo approach of the 1960s through the 1980s where the leading companies provided everything a client company needed, the market today is characterized by companies that specialize in a narrow segment of hardware or software or services. The notion of one company providing everything is not there anymore. The transition point can be traced to the advent of the PC, or personal computer. IBM, always the leader in this market, for the first time broke rank with its own way of doing business and actually let other companies develop key components of its new PC, specifically, the hardware by Intel and the operating system by Microsoft. A compelling visualization of this market shift was presented by Professor Carliss Baldwin of Harvard, part of which is shown in Figure 3.2. The North American industry classification system (NAICS) is the market classification scheme used in the United States, Canada, and Mexico to classify sectors according to the type of manufacturing goods or services they provide. NAICS replaces the older standard industrial classification (SIC).[6]

The diagrams for 1979 and 2005 in Figure 3.2 are provided here together with permission from Professor Baldwin. The Power Point of the entire set of years is available through the URL in the endnote to the figure caption. Figure 3.2 shows the value of the leading providers in the NAICS segments that are related to the computer industry as they progress through the years. What is amazing to note is how IBM, which used to dominate almost all the NAICS codes in the early years, has shifted to focusing on a narrow set of NAICS codes. The few other providers that also provided such a wide range of NAICS codes and that are still around today, such as HP, also went through this transition. As the figure shows, the market today is characterized by the specialization of provider companies into narrow portions of the relevant NAICS codes. No one company can claim to do everything anymore. Cooperation among providers to provide the whole range of products and services, and with it the need to rely on outsourcing, has become a market imperative.

This market transformation is also evident in the transformation of IBM itself, from a proprietary manufacturer of hardware and its accompanying software from 1956 till 1990 to an open structure Internet emphasis between 1990 and 2002 and then to the communization of IT products and the use of open source since 2002. During this transition IBM changed not only its key technological innovations but also its entire business model. In the mainframe era of the 1950s through 1990 IBM's business model was product-centered, and geared toward sales. This silo culture focused on R&D, marketing, and sales. In the 1990 to 2002 period IBM's business model shifted to a service orientation, that is, toward being an integrated solution provider by industry with a culture based on integration and market penetration. This shifted again in 2002

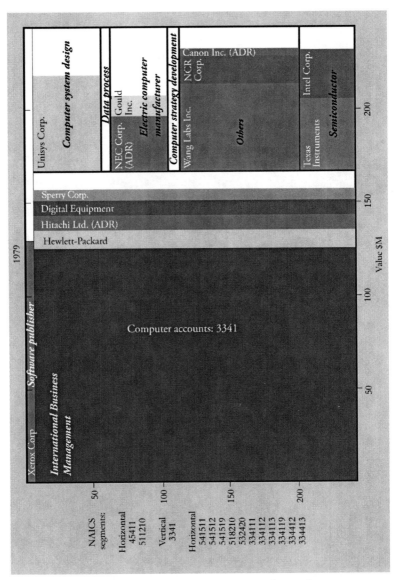

Figure 3.2a. Market valuation of key NAICS codes in the computer industry with list of key providers in 1979 and 2005.[7]

Source: Adapted from Baldwin (n.d.). Used with permission.

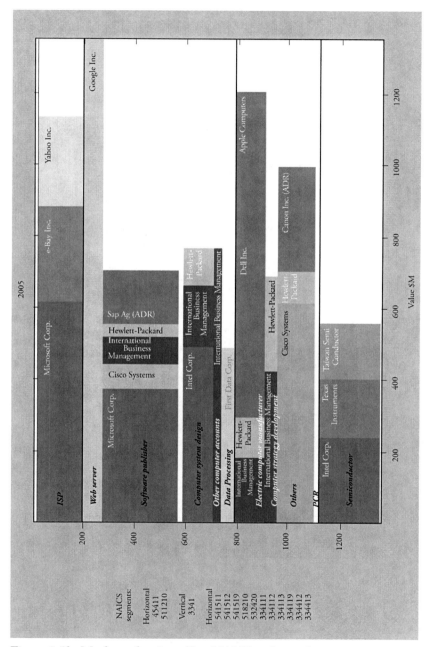

Figure 3.2b. Market valuation of key NAICS codes in the computer industry with list of key providers in 1979 and 2005.[7]

Source: Adapted from Baldwin (n.d.). Used with permission.

when IBM's business model became more globally customer-centered. IBM now provides integrated processes across industries with a culture centered on utilizing its global competencies and ability to innovate in order to provide value to its customers.[8] And, showing how fast the market is continuously changing, IBM's new chief executive officer (CEO) Palmisano is now leading a new shift in strategy: moving from services back to software in response to the market where higher profits can be achieved through harder-to-replicate specialized software. He is intent on doubling earnings by 2015. (In 2010 services were 41% of IBM's operating profits but are expected to be only 38% by 2015.) To do so, IBM plans growth through acquisition of start-ups and the adoption of software as a service (SaaS).[9]

What Market Segmentation Means

This drastic shift in the IT marketplace is symptomatic of Moore's Law. Gordon E. Moore was a co-founder of Intel. In a 1965 paper he predicted that the number of transistors on an integrated circuit would double every 2 years or so. In 1970 Professor Mead of Caltech coined the term "Moore's Law" to describe this apparent market behavior. So consistent has the market trend been since then that Moore's Law has become accepted in the industry as a kind of truth.[10] This tremendous change in hardware capacity has brought with it a shift in what software can do, and with these two changes has come a shift in what organizations and individuals expect and can derive from their information systems.

To demonstrate this rapidity, think about the core of IT: the transistor. The transistor was invented in 1947 by William Shockley, Walter Brattain, and John Bardeen at AT&T's Bell Labs. It replaced the cumbersome, energy-voracious, and fragile vacuum tube. Suddenly a whole new "solid-state" industry was born out of nowhere, delivering never-heard-of-before gadgets such as small radios and other portable electronics. Then in 1971 Intel introduced the 4000 family and in 1972 the 8088 family of microprocessors. Suddenly, a whole new class of products was born, including calculators, computers in cars and dishwashers, functional MRI (fMRI), portable memory universal serial bus (USB), digital video, the Internet, and mobile phones that are actually computers with all the applications computers can run, and the list goes on and on. What is important to remember when reading this partial list is that at no stage could one be certain where things would be going. As a CIO 10 years ago you could not be blamed for not planning ahead for the possibility of marketing on YouTube and SecondLife. The technology and with it the opportunities it brought, when it came, came suddenly.

In practical terms what this extraordinary growth in hardware capacity and software capability means is that managers of IS in organizations face more uncertainty and risk. Basically, companies cannot know what opportunities IT and IS will bring beyond the very short horizon and so cannot plan their IT and IS investment and strategy early enough. The only constant, as the Queen told Alice in Lewis Carroll's *Through the Looking-Glass and What Alice Found There*, is that companies have to run as fast as they can only to stay in one place and "If you want to get somewhere else, you must run at least twice as fast as that!" That running twice as fast is achieved by outsourcing. As a CIO in Arizona told me in 2009, the reason he outsources is not because it saves money, which other CIOs also told me is only a short-term mirage anyway, but because his current in-house IT team could not possibly meet all the needed objectives on time, even if they worked 24/7. Not knowing where IT and IS will go in 2 years' time, and therefore not being able to hire or train personnel in time for the new opportunities IT or IS might bring about, means that companies need to rely on outsourcing, that is, on the purchase of external expertise, to quickly acquire the labor and expertise they do not currently have in-house but that they must have to stay up to date with the current trends in IS. This is one of the key aspects of the *technology imperative* side of outsourcing. Of course, there are other reasons companies outsource apart from the technology imperative, as we discussed in the previous chapters and as we shall discuss in the next ones.

Just as software clients are forced to rely on outsourcing to quickly acquire capabilities they cannot develop fast enough in-house, that is, the technology imperative, the same applies to the technology providers, which is what the market segmentation shown in Figure 3.2 reflects. With IS technology advancing at such a rapid pace, enabled by the exponential increase in computing power reflected in Moore's Law, it makes sense economically for the technology provider to concentrate on that narrow sliver of the market where it has the best advantage, rather than provide everything a client may need. The result is the shift from silos to a segmented market, as shown in Figure 3.2. It also means that the technology imperative applies to the providers of the technology, too. When a provider, now that it does not have expertise in everything, needs to acquire a new expertise quickly, the way to do it is through outsourcing.

As a result of market segmentation and the technology imperative that caused it, not only do the leading provider companies among the NAICS industry codes specialize, but the software vendors and the clients of these vendors and providers do, too. This technology specialization at the vendor and client level also results in increased outsourcing in the market. Once a vendor specializes in a certain type of technology service, this vendor (a) creates expertise that builds on itself and (b) allows it to gain more economies of scale. For example, a company that specializes in fine-tuning IBM's relational DB2 database can afford to hire the best of the best database administrators (DBAs) because it should have enough workload to justify such expensive experts if it can service many clients. Regular clients who only need such specialized DBA services once every few months would not want to hire such expensive DBAs given that they cost so much and that there simply is not enough work for them to do in one company. Moreover, a top-rate DBA would not typically want to work for such a client given that he or she will probably be the only expert on that topic in the company and will not be able to learn from and with other DBAs. This is a major consideration because such expertise has a short life span and must be constantly augmented to stay relevant and marketable. Here, too, one must run as fast as one can just to stay in the lead. Additionally, hiring a top-notch DBA takes a long time. It is not an entry-level assignment, but an expert position that is paid and selected accordingly. Vetting such candidates takes time and, importantly, it takes the kind of expertise many clients simply do not have. Given this lack of knowledge, it makes more sense for the client to buy the DBA services from the vendor who does have the capability to vet and evaluate the claimed expertise of candidate DBAs. All these are examples of expertise that builds on itself. As to economies of scale, the truth in programming is that many of the problems repeat themselves. Solving a problem or developing a unique code may take ages to complete and test the first time, but once the coding has been done, the next time is a simple case of reusing the code and expertise, which takes only a fraction of the time and effort. As a result, it takes the vendor little time and effort to develop code for a new client, given that the vendor has probably done this kind of job many times in the past. It would take the client whose personnel are doing it for the first time much longer. For example, building a new, standard-looking web page, once the exact requirements are known, might take the vendor only a matter of hours considering it has built hundreds of such web pages in the past. All it needs to do is copy an existing template and make minor changes to it. For the client, however, it might take months to gain all the needed expertise and avoid the kind of common mistakes the vendor would never make. With such economies of scale at play and much less technology risk involved, outsourcing makes perfectly good sense. Again, standardization comes into play. The reason the vendor can gain such expertise is that essentially commercial web pages look alike. Develop one, and all you need to do is tweak it to serve another customer.

The market segmentation shown in Figure 3.2 reflects on a provider level the consequences of such expertise that builds on itself and economies of scale. Companies today, including the technology providers in Figure 3.2, specialize in what they do best and buy or contract through outsourcing to acquire the standardized services and products they need ready-made. It makes no sense to invest years of programmer time to develop complex software or engineer time to develop complex hardware when they can be bought standardized and cheaply.

The Move Toward Standardization

Concurrent with this advent of standardization, the type of applications being outsourced has also changed. In the 1960s and 1970s as service bureau applications became standardized, data centers and standardized applications such as payroll were outsourced. This was technology-centric outsourcing of centralized IT doing mainly standardized organizational processes. In the 1980s with the advent of enterprise-wide application through enterprise resource planning (ERP) systems there came also a trend to outsource business-centric activities such as logistics and inventory management systems. Today, with the standardization of e-commerce through Internet applications, as opposed to specialized electronic data interchange (EDI)[11] between specific companies to tie their, and only their, mainframes together, there is a move toward industry-centric outsourcing with online packaged applications and services.[12] If the primary consideration is only financial and the specific type of IT involved is as standardized as a utility then it makes no sense economically to keep it in-house.[13]

The move from technological silos toward horizontal integration among IT providers represents a broad transition in the industry as a whole from *stand-alone* company- and task-specific IT toward *integrated* and *standardized* IT. This transformation is typical of the move of any technology from what the diffusion of innovation theory[14] calls the early adopter phase to the late majority phase, discussed next. This shift is also part of the technological imperative toward outsourcing.

This transition, however, is not easy. It involves changing people's mind-sets and understanding about IT. In a recent roundtable we had with the CIOs in the automotive industry in Detroit in 2007, the assistant to the CIO of one of the big three car manufacturers told us of the problems they were having in making the transition. Over the years their internal clients got so used to having tailor-made and customized IT that when the CIO tried to push toward more standardization and integration so the IT in the various divisions could speak to each other, and as a side bonus to also cut the cost and complexity of maintaining these systems, the managers of these divisions in the company were less than enthusiastic about it. Custom-designed IT can always be better than standardized IT, and once the clients become accustomed to such personalized systems it is hard to wean them off. It takes CIOs with steel in their character to push through such changes, and this automotive assistant CIO certainly gave the impression of having such a character. As we shall discuss in some of the following chapters, taking IT to the next stage of standardization by outsourcing requires even more of a backbone, meaning that the choice of the person to lead the projects is crucial.

Part 2: The Technology Diffusion Model and Attitudes to Technology Risks

Another aspect of the technology imperative behind outsourcing, one that is closely related to how standardized the technology is, is based on Roger's Diffusion of Innovation theory.[15] This theory, although not developed originally for the context of IT, is very applicable to this topic, too.[16] The essence of the theory as it will be adapted in this section to the context of outsourcing is that *new technologies are adopted by different segments of the market at different maturity periods of the technology, and in each maturity period for different reasons.*

Initially, a new technology is adopted by the *innovators*. These are a small segment of the marketplace, maybe accounting for 2.5% of the companies.[17] Innovators adopt the new technology for technology's sake. These companies adopt the technology first when its potential is still unknown. It is almost as though their motto, in the words of *Enterprise-D's* Captain Jean-Luc Picard in *Star Trek*, is "to boldly go where no one has gone before." R&D companies often fit into this category. Artists and scientists are often also in this category. Think of a programmer who is in love with the programming and spends hours trying out obscure options in the software even if these will never be used, just for the fun of it. At the stage when innovators adopt the technology the market for the technology does not yet exist, its business potential is untried, and the technology itself is risky and in its infancy. Only companies that are technologically savvy adopt a new IT at this stage. The risks here are therefore both technological ones and business ones.

Most new IT technologies fail to make it beyond the innovator stage. But some technologies do make it to the next stage. The few that do are adopted by the next segment in the marketplace, the *early adopters*. The early adopters compose maybe the next 13.5% of companies.[18] These are the optimist-pragmatists. They know there is no market yet, but they see the potential this new technology could give them if they adopt it before anyone else does. The early adopters adopt the new technology to create a strategic advantage: to have what no one else has and thereby gain market share. This is a risky business strategy because the market for the new technology is not yet there and therefore its market potential cannot be tested, although the technology risks are much reduced at this stage compared with the innovator stage. This is where Amazon.com was in 1995 when it proposed e-commerce.

Of the few technologies that make it this far to the early adopter stage, most fail to cross over the chasm to the next segment, the *early majority*, which accounts for maybe another 34% of the market.[19] The early majority adopt the new technology based on a calculated business risk assessment. Companies in this segment adopt a new technology because its return on investment (ROI) and other measures of financial risk management justify the risk. This application of risk analysis is possible at this stage because the market for the new technology is now known—having been created by the early adopters—and the technology and investment in it can therefore be evaluated and tested. Note that the early adopters worked with an unknown or even not yet conceived market, so ROI and equivalent measures were not yet possible. At the early majority stage the technology and market are known, so the technology and business risks are much smaller, but so too is the potential for a strategic advantage.

There is a mind-set shift between the innovators and the early adopters on the one hand and the early majority and the rest on the other. The innovators and early adopters are not afraid of change. They actually seek it. This is the attitude one needs to adapt to the constantly changing world of IT and the IS it enables where change is continuous. The early majority and others are wary of change. They certainly do not seek it because change means more risks, and these risks are often unknown or unknowable risks. These early majority managers do not want to make this additional change unless there is a really compelling reason to do so, nor do, perhaps, the rest of the managers. This amounts to a mind-set chasm between the early adopters and the early majority. The early adopters operate in an unknown market. They cannot go and do market research before deciding whether to adopt the new technology because the market simply is not there yet. In contrast, the early majority operate in a known market with a proven technology.[20] The early majority can and do adopt the mantra of "do your homework before you make a decision." To the early majority it is all about measuring and controlling risk. The early adopters can only guess.

The story of Xerox and IBM is telling in this regard.[21] In the 1950s Xerox started developing a new revolutionary machine: the photocopying machine. This was a revolutionary idea back in the 1950s. In the 1950s when a manager wanted to make a copy of a document he would send it with a gofer to the secretaries. (A secretary in the English of the 1950s was mostly a woman who was employed to type on a typewriter.) The secretary would type the document, maybe adding carbon paper to make two or three additional copies or using a stencil to type it into wax paper so many copies could be cranked out. This process would take some time, but no one was in the kind of rush business is in today. Xerox, running into financial difficulties, suggested the patent to IBM. IBM, being a well-run business in the early majority segment, hired ADL, a consulting firm, to do market research for them to learn the market potential of this new invention. ADL examined the existing market and then concluded that the investment in photocopying could not possibly be justified even if photocopying were to capture all the carbon paper and other copying tool markets of the time. Using photocopying to copy pictures and diagrams was not even suggested. IBM therefore refused to buy the patent and Xerox went on to become a very successful company and to even coin a new verb in the English language, "to Xerox." Photocopying, or "Xeroxing," was a success, not only because it reduced the need for secretaries, the early majority criterion for success, but also because it created a whole new market that had never existed before, which is the early adopter criterion.

After the early majority, and once a technology has become established and its business potential is no longer in doubt, the technology is adopted by the next segment of the market, the *late majority*. The late majority makes up about another 34% of the market.[22] The mind-set of the late majority is one of risk aversion: New technology is adopted at the stage when it has become a market standard. The new technology and its market are now well known and it is a matter of having it or being out of the mainstream of the business. Last, or maybe not at all, the *laggards* adopt the new technology.

The transformation of e-commerce is also telling in this regard. In 1995 when Amazon.com came out with the concept of selling books through an online store it was a revolutionary idea. Companies had sold through catalogs for years, but taking it online was a new technology. Amazon.com as an early adopter gambled on a new market emerging out of nowhere. Today, e-commerce is in the late majority segment of the market. Even small companies have their own websites, and the look and process of selling is standardized from escrow accounts to PayPal to trust certifications. In fact, it is so standardized that many websites that sell products use the same patented shopping cart icon with the same process behind it (the patent belongs to Amazon.com) to manage their ordering and payments. It is fully standardized and in the category of "have it or lose business." Having a website today is not a gamble on a new technology, so it is not in the realm of the early adopters. It does not even require

ROI to justify investing in it, so it is not in the realm of the early majority either. It is a utility like having phone service. It is squarely in the late majority segment, and, reemphasizing the speed of revolutions in IT, it got there in less than 5 years.

Technology Maturity and Risk

The technology maturity levels in the diffusion of innovation theory[23] have importance also in the context of outsourcing. As always, it is all about mapping and controlling risks, and each stage in the diffusion of innovation has its own unique objectives and risks when it comes to outsourcing.

Innovators are special. To them, business and technology risks are not a primary concern. When innovators outsource it is to gain expertise they do not have in order to understand the technology better.

Among early adopters there is risk awareness, but it is also about opportunities. When early adopters outsource it is in accordance with their objectives. When these companies outsource they do so to gain assets and capabilities they do not yet have. In doing so, they knowingly take a risk, hoping to gain enough strategic advantage to justify the costs of acquiring these assets and knowledge. But this risk is a *gamble*. It is not a calculated risk because the market is not there. They are gambling on something they must yet create.

The early majority mind-set is about ROI, improving current processes, and costs savings considering the risks. These companies outsource accordingly with a view to cut costs and improve processes, which is a very different mind-set from that of the early adopters who are after a strategic advantage. This is more about operational and financial risks and less about technological risks. The early majority manager attempts to learn the market and technology and then *control* the risks. They do not want to gamble; they seek calculated business risks.

The attitude of the late majority is one of risk avoidance. They would rather, figuratively speaking, avoid rocking the boat—but they are not disassociated from the world of business. If a new standard has emerged and that is now the way business is done, then they will adapt and adopt it. To the late majority, outsourcing is about acquiring a standardized technology everyone is using, a technology they too need to adapt if they want to stay in the game. It is not about risk anymore. It is about outsourcing as a business imperative. These are often the bandwagon goers discussed earlier. They outsource because outsourcing has become a standard.

So, to summarize, the attitude toward outsourcing changes from one of risk seeking in an attempt to identify new capabilities and with them strategic advantage among early adopters, to one of seeking calculated risks with the intention of increasing profit and improving processes with proven technology among the early majority, to one of adapting to new standards (because everyone does it) among the late majority, where risk due to outsourcing is not the main concern.

Back to IS and Outsourcing

Diffusion of innovation provides some interesting insights into the risk-taking or risk-avoiding behavior of companies when they outsource. The case with IS outsourcing, however, is more complex. In the case of IS in an organizational setting, there are many stakeholders scattered about the various maturity levels of the technology. These stakeholders are using the technology for their own purposes and therefore have very different objectives and attitudes toward risk. First, there are the techies: the programmers, DBAs, network managers, and so on. They want to try new technologies regardless of the business implications. To these innovators, outsourcing to gain access to a new technology is interesting—and it promotes their business value if they are up to date with these new technologies. If outsourcing means bringing in new technology without risking their jobs then they will be interested.

In contrast to these innovators who are eager to try new IT regardless of risks, many non-IT managers care primarily about meeting the quotas and critical success factor (CSF) numbers they are responsible for. They do not care about innovations in the IT as such. They are very much risk conscious. They are conscious about their own responsibility to manage production or service up to the required code, and they are very conscious about the additional risks of trying out new technologies. All they want from the IT is for it to help them achieve their quotas better. They do not want to try anything new, IT or no IT, unless it is proven and can contribute to their specific CSF numbers. To them, any change in the IT, whether a new system or outsourcing an existing one, means taking additional operational risks about something they do not understand and maybe do not even need. Besides, if something goes wrong with the new IT they will have to pay the price in delayed operations and quality control problems, and if the new IT is a success then it will not be to their credit anyway. And so, when it concerns IT, these managers are in the early majority mind-set. Show them the "what's in it for me" in the outsourcing process and then, if their own risk analysis as far as providing the goods and services they are responsible for is favorable (and this is not the same as the outsourced IT itself), they will consider it. Other managers are in the late majority category. They will only adopt a change if ordered to do so.

In between these two groups are IS management who are in charge of the IT and of IT outsourcing contracts. The mind-set of these IS managers concerning IT is also mostly one of an early majority, that is, controlling the risks, but their risks are not the same risks as those of the non-IT managers. Non-IT managers are in charge of the goods and services and care about the IT only to the extent that it affects any of those. IT managers are in charge of providing IT services to the rest of the organization, preferably in as much a standardized IT fashion as possible. (There is also the chief financial officer [CFO], who is concerned with financial risks, but more on that topic in another chapter.) In outsourcing the IT or part of it, the risks the non-IT managers care about are therefore mainly in terms of goods and services quality and schedule problems caused by the new IT or by outsourcing the IT services. In contrast, to the IT managers the risks are first of all about choosing the right vendor and the right IT (and these IT change drastically every few years) and then dealing with the implementation issues—all these problems precede the quality and schedule problems of the non-IT managers. Additionally, every so often the IT managers also take the position of an early adopter: seeking to gain competitive advantages for the organization through the outsourced IT. These risks the IT managers have are compounded by the concurrent need to hold back the innovators (such as the programmers and other technical staff) who want to push ahead even when the technology is not relevant and who do not understand the business risks involved.

These risk differences tie back to another reason why IT management and its outsourcing are unique. Although as an IS manager most of the problems you face are in the early majority segments of the diffusion of innovation, you will also make many early adopter type decisions—and by far many more than other managers do, precisely because IT is changing so rapidly and these changes often represent a revolution rather than evolution of technology. Your objective when encountering a new IS technology is to seek risk rather than to control risk, which is what other managers usually do, because of the potential new IS technologies bring and because you do not want to be too late in adopting these new technologies. To an IS manager such an early adopter decision may need to be made once or twice a year (currently, the key questions are about Cloud computing and mobile computing). To non-IS managers, in contrast, such an early adopter decision may be made once or twice in a career, if at all. This is a crucial difference. Early adopter decisions are unstructured and seek risk, while early majority decision making is mostly structured: Mistakes can be mostly corrected, and the objective is to control risk.

The decision to outsource IS, then, depends not only on the maturity of the specific technology but also on convincing and managing the different stakeholders who themselves are at different stages of the technology maturity. The IS management may be an early adopter, but they may need to contend with non-IS managers whose mind-set is an early or even a late majority.

Cloud Computing and the Diffusion of IT Innovation

A determining characteristic of when an IT reaches the late majority segment is the emergence, and then dominance, of standards. This is why Carr[24] claims IT is mostly in the late majority segment. Showing how fast this transition is now happening, although Cloud computing is still a work in progress according to the U.S. government agency in charge,[25] the industry is already defining standards that will allow companies to integrate their Cloud components.[26]

Of Revolutions and Evolutions in IT

To clarify the difference between revolution and evolution, think of the transition from a feather to a fountain pen and then to a ballpoint pen. That was evolution. Throughout this transition the nature of the task did not change even as the technology got better. One still wrote and thought with a pen as one did with a feather, one word at a time to make one sentence at a time. The transition from a pen to a word-processor, on the other hand, was a revolution. Suddenly text could be reused, corrected in place, copied and pasted, and have its font changed. Words and sentences could be inserted without retyping the following text, existing documents could be updated and shared, inter-active features could be added to the text, and the IT could automatically correct spelling, perform dynamic and automatic tabulation, and so on. The whole process of writing documents and using them became totally different.

This transition is indicative of the nature of IT. IT has been going through a revolution, a paradigm change, every 5 years or so since commercial computing began around 1958. The IT industry in the 1960s was characterized by companies investing less than 5% of capital expenditure on their IT. It was treated by many as a "novel idea." The technology itself was characterized by its hardware, the mainframe. The key to understanding the mainframe mentality of those of us who lived through it is not so much its technical prowess, or maybe lack thereof in many of the real-time user interface aspects we have become accustomed to in the 2000s, but rather the programming and management philosophy it was based on and inspired. This was a centralized system, and the way it was run, both internally in its operating system and the programming languages it employed, and externally in the structure of the all-powerful IT department that ran it, was a hierarchy. The types of applications it ran, initially systems such as payroll and logistics, were also fully standardized and centralized types of systems. Mainframes cost a fortune and would occupy whole halls, but their use was not really strategic. Rather, it was to provide better and cheaper standardized "factory" type applications of the payroll type that could now be run by several IT technicians faster and with fewer mistakes than by hundreds of accountants. This is IT geared toward the late majority segment.

Skip a few years forward to the 1970s, and mainframes have changed from being stand-alone giants to becoming part of interconnected networks of even stronger and more powerful mainframes. This was a paradigm shift in both technology and its application. Leading thinkers in the 1970s started talking about the strategic advantage companies could glean from their IT and how it could do more than just automate the standardized organizational operations of the payroll type.[27] This was IT espoused as it might be geared toward the early adopters segment. During the 1970s, companies invested about 30% of their capital expenditure on their IT.

Next came the PC revolution of the 1980s and with it a shift toward personal computing, and then the network revolution of the 1990s connecting PCs with mainframes in client-server architectures, and then the ubiquitous computing of the 2000s with the Internet, and then smart phones running apps as powerful as PCs used to be, and the list will probably go on. With each new revolution, new opportunities that nobody dreamt of became commonly used. With each new revolution, new business applications became possible. And with each new revolution there was a scramble by companies to quickly take advantage of the new technology to gain strategic advantage by relying on outsourcing to quickly fill in the gaps in their capability as early adopters; or, to take advantage of whatever had already become the new market through outsourcing on a calculated risk basis after the market was established as early majority; or, adapting to the new standards the market created by outsourcing to acquire what by then had become standardized services as late majority simply to stay in business without any risk calculations.

Tying It All Together

The key to correct outsourcing, then, apart from knowing your risks and controlling them as discussed in the previous chapters, and apart from the financial bottom line cost issues that are always important, is to know where your company stands and where those you serve in the organization stand on the diffusion of innovation graph.

IS technology is changing at such a rapid rate that companies cannot be experts in everything, not even the leading software provider giants of yesteryear. The rapid change also means that companies cannot plan ahead of time by hiring a new workforce or training their current workforce in order to acquire all possibly needed future capabilities in-house. With such rapid change it is unknown where the market will go and what capabilities might be needed. So, once they are faced with this need, companies must resort to acquiring these new technology capabilities from other companies, that is, they need to outsource to acquire expertise. This is the technology imperative: outsourcing as a way to quickly acquire expert capabilities from outside the company. Companies may not have been able to see this need ahead of time because of the speed with which new technologies and the possibilities they create became available.

Supporting this trend is the shift in much of the IT market toward the standardization characterized by an early and late majority-oriented market. Standardization allows for cross-company IT standards and protocols, making it possible for clients not to rely on a single provider. Indeed, the breakup of the silo-oriented market of the 1960s and 1970s into the segments market of the 1990s and 2000s forced technology providers as well to seek such IT standards and protocols so they could concentrate on their own sliver of the market by relying on complementary services of other companies.

Pharmaceutical Example

This is a story told to me by the CFO of Élan in the summer of 2009. It also appears on the web. Élan is an Irish pharmaceutical company that produces bapineuzumab, which "appears to slow the devastating effects of Alzheimer's."[28] There are currently four drugs that treat Alzheimer's. Each is effective in only about 30% of the patients. Bapineuzumab has the potential to become a market blockbuster, is effective in about 70% of cases, and may actually reverse Alzheimer's. The drug is currently in Phase 3 testing.[29] In 2007 during the banking meltdown Élan ran into cash flow problems and requested 30 multinationals to submit suggestions for creating an alliance with them. Élan chose Johnson & Johnson because the two companies had a similar organizational culture. Many of their Irish managers had spent many years in the United States and the scientists in both companies had rapport with each other. Johnson & Johnson agreed to invest €1.5 billion in a joint venture to take this drug to the next stage.

Now, let us imagine what an innovator, early adopter, and early majority at Johnson & Johnson might say about such an interfirm alliance. (We shall discuss this as one form of outsourcing.) Think of the innovator as a scientist who is looking at this new medication that, according to initial Phase 2 trials, might reverse, maybe even cure, Alzheimer's. To such a scientist this is about the joy of scientific discovery and knowing the team is doing something really important for humanity. It is true that innovators are aware of the financial potential too but, probably like Jonas Salk who invented the polio vaccine, their primary concern is not the money.[30] An early adopter at Johnson & Johnson, in contrast, might take a different stand. An early adopter may say that if we can come up with an effective medicine for Alzheimer's then we have a blockbuster, and one that cannot be duplicated as a generic for many years to come. This could make Johnson & Johnson the leading pharmaceutical company in the world. The developmental risks are high and obviously should never be ignored, but, all in all, these risks, even if we cannot quantify them, are justified. This is a calculated gamble. An early majority manager at Johnson & Johnson, however, would be very cautious: €1.5 billion is a lot of money, and even a large company such as Johnson & Johnson could be fatally hurt if it lost so much. Moreover, the risks cannot be quantified or measured. And, this early majority manager will remind us, while there is certainly a market for such a drug, this drug might not be the right one. So, really, the market is not necessarily there. And so such an early majority person would say, "Wait. Calm down. There is still Phase 3 and there is still the FDA, and even then approved drugs have been pulled off the market by the FDA after they were approved because of side effects. Let us calculate the risk and the potential. We have seen many promising Phase 2 medications either fail to make it through Phase 3 or be recalled. True, this may be a blockbuster as the early adopter said, and, yes, we are doing something really important for humanity. It is interesting as the innovator thinks and it is obviously also important, but we cannot afford to gamble the company on it." Different stakeholders are on different segments of the technology diffusion graph.

IT Does Matter; It Just Matters When You Ask

The discussion on market segmentation and technology standardization combined with the discussion on the diffusion of innovation relates directly to an important raging debate about the importance of IT. In 2003 Carr suggested in a *Harvard Business Review* article that "IT Doesn't Matter."[31] In a nutshell, Carr says that IT has become ubiquitous and an essential backbone of business. It is a critical resource. Indeed, investment in IT went up from 5% in the 1960s to 15% in the 1980s, to 30% in the 1990s, and to 50% currently. IT today, in contrast to the 1960s, is used by everyone, including senior managers who make decisions. But if IT is ubiquitous then it cannot anymore create strategic advantage. Resources provide a strategic advantage when only a few companies have them, but when a resource becomes a crucial necessity to business and everyone has it, as IT is today, then it is a necessary cost to be reckoned with but not an advantage. Carr therefore differentiates between a *proprietary technology*, which is owned and applied exclusively by a single company to create a strategic advantage, and an *infrastructure technology*, which is a common technology all players have access to and which is governed by standards and a leveled playing field. Microsoft Windows is a proprietary technology. Having a website to sell your merchandise online is an infrastructure technology. Proprietary technologies can provide strategic advantage, but the window of opportunity for a proprietary technology today is mostly very small as new ITs move quickly from the proprietary to the standardized infrastructure category. Therefore, says Carr, rather than invest in the risky proprietary technology, it is cheaper and better to wait and then buy ready-made infrastructure IT. As such, recommends Carr, companies should treat their IT in the same manner as they treat their other utilities. Companies should buy it from a vendor who specializes in that specific utility. In other words, Carr recommends outsourcing IT and in doing so move from an offensive to a defensive strategy by concentrating on the risks and price rather than on the potential advantages. Basically, says Carr, it is better to be a follower in IT strategy than a leader because leaders waste resources in trying to be ahead of the curve. Indeed, between 1999 and 2001 U.S. companies spent $130 million on IT they never used.[32]

Notice that Carr,[33] recognizing the segmentation and standardization in the market, is taking the position of a late majority manager. Indeed, much criticism has been leveled on Carr on account of his degrading view of IS—interestingly, Carr is not an IS manager or researcher while many of those who criticize him are. Schrage, co-director of the MIT Media Lab's eMarkets Initiative, rebuts that capital is also a ubiquitous commodity, but give a company $100 million, and it will be able to use it to create a competitive advantage. It is not about the availability of the commodity alone that counts but rather about how it is used.[34] Or perhaps the following is a more accurate statement: Money, or IT, does not solve all the problems of a company, but the lack of it certainly creates many of them. IT can be treated as a standard tool and should therefore be outsourced as a standardized process with cost-cutting as a primary objective, in the view of Carr as an early majority person, but it can also transform the organization, in the view of a CIO who is an early adopter, by making good management better and bad management worse, and should therefore be outsourced, if at all, for the acquisition of capabilities outsourcing brings. After all, IT is the nervous system of the company; outsourcing it is seldom a stand-alone issue.

Another point worth mentioning about Carr[35] is that the approach he champions is that of traditional outsourcing. Traditional outsourcing in the 1960s and 1970s was technology centric and dealt with service bureau centralized applications such as payroll IS and data centers IT. Whether this applies to the transition IS outsourcing made in the 1980s[36] toward distributed enterprise applications, such as the ERP system, or the remote outsourcing currently under way, is an open question. At any rate, IS outsourcing should be done with the realization that IS are the nervous system of the company with all the risks this entails and that different kinds of IT have different kinds of impact on the organization.[37] Not all IS are borne the same, and should not be outsourced the same either.

This means knowing whether companies need to know where they stand on each particular IS technology. The question is (a) are you seeking capabilities to gain strategic advantage ahead of the market with non-standardized technology as an early adopter and in doing so behaving as an early adopter cautious risk seeker, or (b) are you seeking to improve your current standing while controlling your risks based on market analysis as an early majority person, or (c) are you seeking to catch up with standardized routine technology because you have to do so as a late majority person à la Carr?[38] Each of these segments outsources for different reasons and thus faces different risks.

In Lieu of a Boilerplate

In continuation of the structured guidelines in the previous chapter, here are more steps to follow as discussed in this chapter.

Step 3: Know Where You Stand With the Technology

1. Know if the technology you need to acquire through outsourcing is standard or is new and, importantly, whether your organization plans to use it in the standard way the market currently uses such IS. These considerations will make a big difference in the risks your organization will face when it outsources and in how the IS processes are going to be managed.

   - If the IS are as standardized as those of a utility service, then buying the IS ready-made as Carr suggests may be the best option.[39] There is no reason to assume the IS can provide a strategic advantage, so it is cheaper and faster and the quality is better guaranteed by buying it ready-made. Outsourcing e-mail and the management of gigabytes of memory are true candidates for such activities, but only if the vendor can provide secure and reliable services throughout the expected service period and complies with government regulations, such as privacy.

   - If, at the other extreme, the IS are uniquely special and may provide a strategic advantage, then your IT does matter, and outsourcing in the fashion of buying ready-made IS may not be the best way to go about it. Banks typically prefer to keep their proprietary software in-house because, among other reasons, of risks of ownership.

   - Be aware, however, that IS rarely fall into one of those two extremes. It is usually a matter of trade-offs of different kinds of risks and opportunities.

2. Know if this technology for your company is in the realm of the innovator, early adopter, early majority, or late majority—and manage its outsourcing accordingly. This too will determine the types and levels of risk you can expect to face.

   - Early adopters face the risks of an unknown technology and how the market will respond to it. These managers are not risk averse. To these adopters, the recommendation made by Carr is irrelevant.[40] Outsourcing here as a way of acquiring expertise may be an option.

   - Early majority managers know, or at least think they know, their risks, so their mind-set is one of controlling risks. These risks are mainly financial ones; therefore, outsourcing here as a way of cutting costs may be an option.

- Late majority managers are risk averse. They adopt the IS when they have become a standard way of doing business. By the time these managers adopt the IS, these IS have become standardized and readily available as ready-made packages. Late majority managers should consider outsourcing on a fixed price basis to acquire the IS as a utility as Carr suggests.[41]

3. Be sure to treat technology evolution as evolution, but treat technology revolution with extra caution. There is more risk in revolutions because one knows where they begin but not where they go from there, and revolutions tend to consume and destroy those that take part in them. As Christensen[42] describes the hard-drive technology changes in the 1990s, with each new revolutionary breakthrough in technology all the previous leading companies, except for IBM, went out of business.

4. As in the previous chapters, remember, it is all about recognizing and then controlling risks. The risks are going to be different depending on where you stand and where you are going.

CHAPTER 4

Agency and Outsourcing Risk Management

"Would you tell me, please, which way I ought to go from here?"
"That depends a good deal on where you want to get to," said the Cat.
"I don't much care where—" said Alice.
"Then it doesn't matter which way you go," said the Cat.
"—so long as I get SOMEWHERE," Alice added as an explanation.
"Oh, you're sure to do that," said the Cat, "if you only walk long enough."

—Lewis Carroll, *Alice's Adventures in Wonderland*, chapter 6.

Back to the Main Question

In a recent industry survey of 366 business technology professionals published by *Information Week*, 7% of the respondents said their company's approach to outsourcing its information technology (IT) is to outsource as much as possible; another 23% said the policy is to outsource as much as possible except for executive and managerial positions; another 21% said it is to outsource as much as possible except for executive, managerial, and engineering positions; and another 8% said the same but added except for development roles.[1] This adds up to 59% of companies that would outsource regardless of the nature of the IT and the task. With such an attitude toward wholesale IT outsourcing it may indeed be that Carr[2] was right when he predicted that IT should be treated as a utility and outsourced except in special cases. And yet, things are really not that simple. Forty-three percent of the respondents to the *Information Week* survey also said their company did not have a system in place to manage their information systems (IS) outsourcing vendors.[3] And this brings us back to the story in the Prologue of the chief information officer (CIO) sitting in his office outside Detroit commiserating that he outsources his IT all the time but has no idea if he is doing it correctly. If he were one of those 59% then he was in for a nasty surprise. And he was; he was transferred to another position shortly afterwards. Outsourcing is not that simple.

The real question the CIO should have been asking himself was whether his objective in IS outsourcing was about better allocating risks, costs, and resources constructively after thoughtful analysis or was it perhaps only about abrogating responsibility. This means first and foremost understanding and managing the risks. It is after all *the main responsibility of a manager to control and if control is impossible then at least to manage risks*. A convenient way of understating the context of these risks is through "agency theory." Only after the various risks have been brought to acceptable levels do other considerations, such as new IS initiatives and opportunities, come into play.

Agency Theory

One of the most popular theories academics have to explain outsourcing, and indeed contracting with other companies in general, is agency theory.[4] Agency theory, and its derivative contract theory,[5] in a nutshell, deal with the case of a *principal* who lets out work to an *agent* who then performs it. Within this context the principal faces an *agency problem*, which boils down to the issue that there is no way the principal can know as much about the agent and the work it is supposed to be doing as the agent itself knows. This *information asymmetry*, whereby the agent knows more than the principal does and may take advantage of this to advance its own interests, which may well be quite different from those of the principal, translates into three categories of risks: *adverse selection* risks, *moral hazard* risks, and *unexpected contingencies* risks. In the context of outsourcing the principal is the client company and the agent is the vendor company. At the core of agency is the concern to minimize the loss a principal may encounter as a result of the agent having its own interests rather than those of the principal at heart,[6] and the realization that because of these conflicting interests information asymmetry increases the principal's risks.[7] As the chief executive officer (CEO) of Zappos, an online shoe selling company, put it in reflecting about the mistakes his company made in outsourcing: "Trusting that a third party would care about our customers as much as we did was one of our biggest mistakes."[8] Agency theory has been extensively applied to explain the details of IS outsourcing.[9] Understanding the agency relationship is crucial because many outsourcing projects, estimated by some at 28%,[10] fail because of contractual management issues.

Managing Adverse Selection Risks

Adverse selection risks deal with identifying trustworthy agents before the contract is signed and, importantly, avoiding the risky others. Chronologically within the outsourcing process this happens after the outsourcing client (the principal) has decided what the extent of the outsourced project will be, estimated the range of cost it is willing to pay, secured the funds, and issued a tender (otherwise known as an RFP, the acronym for request for proposals). Once this RFP has been issued, and vendors start bidding on it, the principal needs to choose among the contending vendors (agents). The principal's problem is that unless proper steps are taken, such as choosing only among vendors the client has contracted with in the past or only among appropriately certified vendors, the competing agents can masquerade as almost anything they wish and can claim to be able to do more than they really can.

The principal needs to be careful in its choice of an agent—and this is adverse selection risk. Choosing the wrong agent not only may delay the project but also may cause additional expensive collateral damage. Take the large European bank discussed in Gefen and colleagues[11] as an example. The bank adheres to the regulations issued by the governments and central banks in the countries it operates in, including the Federal Reserve in the United States and the European Central Bank in the EU. Adhering to these regulations translates among other things to software modification. Choosing the wrong vendor might mean not only delays in implementing these regulations, and the subsequent fines from the central banks, but also the risk of corrupting the data because of glitches in the developed software. Correcting data after such a glitch is not easy or straightforward because the bank is not allowed to just change the balance sheets of its clients. With all this in mind, choosing the right agent is crucial and is treated accordingly.

Throughout this agent selection process the principal typically does not have all the information it needs about the agents who are bidding on the tender—and this poses a unique set of risks that CIOs are eager to avoid. Indeed, in my talks with CIOs they often emphasize that they outsource only to a select few vendors—and the CIOs make sure these few vendors realize how special and profitable to them this relationship is so they invest over and above so as not to lose this privilege. This, in effect, creates a select club of vendors who have a strong vested interest in maintaining this relationship. These vendors, as I can testify from my own past experience as a project manager in one of them, will do within reason all that is necessary to make sure the project succeeds, even going more than the extra mile beyond what the contract says to make sure the principal is satisfied. After all, at stake here is not only this project but also their entire long-term relationship with the client. In other cases with big client companies, the client's IS managers will reward those vendors who have been delivering to their satisfaction over the long run with the easier-to-manage and less-risky time and materials contracts.[12] Other ways of managing adverse selection risks in an IS outsourcing relationship include preferring vendors based on recommendations either from other clients or, better still, based on previous contracts the particular vendor had with the client.[13] Another way to preselect a short list of trusted vendors is by relying on certification from appropriate agencies.[14]

It is all about creating incentives that will first of all cause the vendor to not want to take advantage of its information symmetry, either by bidding on an RFP it cannot deliver on or by not completing the work. This is also a matter of managing trust and creating a trustworthy relationship between the client and the vendor.[15] Trust-based relationships add special extra value to the business relationship because both sides know the other is also in it for the long run and is unlikely therefore to rush to take opportunistic advantage of the situation. It also means both sides know that in the long run it is not a zero-sum game between them. Having such a trusting relationship allows companies to somewhat let their guard down a bit so to speak and not be on constant vigilance with all the extra costs this brings about.

Moral Hazard Risks

Once the contract has been signed and the agent starts working on the contract the principal faces a new set of risks known as *moral hazard risks*. These risks amount to not knowing exactly what the agent is doing, not knowing the quality of its work and how the agent is doing this work, not knowing what quality controls the agent has and whether the agent is really applying them, and not knowing whether or not the agent will meet the timetables. The key issue here is to identify problems early on and take steps, preferably in coordination with the agent, to remedy the problems before things get out of control.

It is important to note here that this does not necessarily mean that the vendor is malicious, bad intentioned, or cannot be trusted or that therefore steps should be taken to curb the agent. On the contrary, the vendor too wants the project to succeed and will reasonably invest in its success, at least as long as it is not actually losing money on it. But the vendor has its own motives, objectives, and understanding of how things should be done. Moreover, the vendor is legally bound first and foremost to serve its shareholders and make a profit. So there is nothing wrong, and it is to be expected, that the principal and the agent will have different objectives, as long as all parties realize this and take steps to reduce the risks it may cause. After all, even within the same organization there are disagreements among departments, especially the IT department.

Even with strict formal contracting moral hazard remains a serious risk because, in a large IS development of any kind, so many things cannot be made explicit enough in a contract. Indeed, so many things cannot be known well enough by the client when the requirements document and with it the tender are made. And this is true even more in the case of outsourcing, because the agent has a vested interest to hide its problems. Agents do not like it when the principal tries to micromanage or micromonitor their activities. And that is precisely what happens when the principal starts suspecting the agent is having trouble, because any problems the agent cannot resolve will be the principal's problems, too. And so, when schedule is not met, or a glitch is found, or key personnel leave or need to be moved to a more urgent project, or the technology does not perform as expected, or any of a myriad of other problems occur during development and testing, the agent has a strong incentive not to report it to the principal but rather to try and solve the problem quietly. And then the agent may try to cut corners where the principal cannot easily notice (such as in quality control and testing) in order to save time and money, as well as the wrath of an inexperienced principal when the schedule is not met to perfection. Unless the principal takes explicit steps to control such risks (i.e., the agent taking advantage of its information asymmetry) there is little chance the principal could know about it, especially if the agent is offshore.

Moral hazard risks must be accounted for, and not only because the agent may have a reason to cover up. It is important to reemphasize again the analogy of IS projects to jigsaw puzzles. It is not uncommon for the requirements for such projects to span thousands of pages, and so it is almost impossible for most people to comprehend all the details in such large documents, let alone identify where the details contradict each other or current practices. It is not until almost all the pieces of an IS project jigsaw are in place that people start seeing what pieces are missing and what pieces need to be reshaped so everything fits in nicely.[16] This problem is, of course, aggravated when the IS project is outsourced and the people developing the software do not even belong to the same organization and do not share the same business culture and knowledge with those using the software. This problem is exacerbated even more when the project is cut in size, as it often is, to meet budgetary constraints after the original requirements are approved. In such cases sections are often cut out without fully understanding how the removal of a function may affect other parts of the system. It is only when all the parts of the software project are put together that the implications of the missing sections become obvious, by which time one has to be careful not to have the project digress into a blame war between the principal and the agent. Being fully aware of what the agent is doing is crucial even though the agent is doing nothing wrong, because the agent can notice earlier on what mistakes the principal made, and identifying these problems early can help in alleviating them.

Managing Moral Hazard Risks

Moral hazard risks are unavoidable, but steps can be taken to mitigate them. The first step clients can take to reduce or at least control these risks is to add procedures and processes to *measure* what is going on. Measuring what is happening is an imperative step in handling any kind of project. As Peter Drucker famously said, "If you can't measure it, you can't manage it,"[17] or as Lord Kelvin (Sir William Tompson) said earlier about science, "When you can measure what you are speaking about, and express it in numbers, you know something about it; but when you cannot measure it, when you cannot express it in numbers, your knowledge is of a meagre and unsatisfactory kind."[18] To measure in this case means to (a) identify the critical success factors (CSFs) at every milestone in the project, (b) assign *measurable critical values* of when there is trouble to every one of these CSFs, and (c) to determine how and how often this measurement should be done. Once this measurement system is in place the principal can figuratively keep its finger on the pulse of the project and know early enough if something is amiss. Without continuous measurement keeping track, and more importantly keeping an early warning system up and running, would be impossible. This is, of course, true of any type of management, but it is even more critical in the case of IS outsourcing because the principal is not there on site all the time and so really does not know what is happening. Moreover, measuring these CSFs not only sends a message to the agent that the principal is involved and cares about the project but also tells the agent what aspects of the project are most important to the principal.

Measuring is closely coupled with another step principals can take, which is *monitoring*. Monitoring can take several forms. To being with, as an integral part of any outsourcing project the client should insist that the vendor report on these CSFs regularly and automatically whenever a CSF measure reaches a critical value. This should be in the contract. Thus, for example, the contract should stipulate that there will be a periodic progress report from the agent, as well as a report when any quality control measure exceeds its CSF critical value. These progress reports could be addressed weekly or biweekly to tactical project management and monthly or bimonthly to senior management. Monitoring is crucial for success in outsourcing, which is not about abrogating responsibility but rather about letting someone else do the work, someone who can do it faster, better, or cheaper. Monitoring, therefore, is a crucial way of not abrogating this responsibility. And, perhaps not less important, monitoring is also a message the principal sends the agent that there is no free lunch! Monitoring may also include the on-site presence of a principal's liaison officer who is embedded in the projects the agent is running for the principal. This could give the principal firsthand information about what is happening and why, beyond the periodic reporting. And, moreover, when the agent runs into difficulties in understanding what the principal wants, which should not be ruled out, this liaison can quickly fill in the gaps or at least know who to contact on the principal's side to get things moving quickly. Indeed, being on-site and therefore having someone embedded with the vendor, especially when the vendor is in another country, has been shown to improve project success.[19] It also creates a better sense of being one team with the developers, which also contributes to project success because the parties understand each other better and realize it is a joint project whose success requires everyone to play their part.[20] This also broadcasts to the agent how seriously the principal takes the project.

As important as monitoring is, it is also important not to cross the line. The principal and agent should agree ahead of time in the contract itself on what is being measured and how frequently. This also sends a message to the agent that the principal is not micromanaging the relationship. After all, as a principal you want the agent to take responsibility and enjoy their work. Even with the best of monitoring, there will still be moral hazard risk, so you really want the agent on your side. And so measurement and monitoring by the principal should be thought of not only as a tool for controlling the principal's risks, which it is, but also as a way to broadcast to the agent exactly what the principal wants and let the agent know how the principal wants the relationship to be managed. Setting the rules of the business relationship this way should also reduce misunderstandings and inadvertent border crossings. As a principal, when you set the monitoring standards it is important to remember that the agent does have its own objectives and these are not the same as yours and indeed cannot be so legally because the agent owes its loyalty to its shareholders. Setting the monitoring rules and standards upfront before the contract is signed defines this borderline. Good fences make good neighbors. The risk of micromanaging is convincingly presented by Tiwana and Keil,[21] who show that, based on 57 outsourced and 79 internal IS projects, applying a lot of control may be beneficial in internal IS projects but is detrimental in outsourced ones.

As important as monitoring is, having *meetings* with the agent is also crucial. Periodic meetings serve to bolster monitoring, but they also serve a possibly even more important role in *building trust* and creating a sense of togetherness, of being one team. Even when there is strict formal contracting, trust remains a crucial element in outsourcing IS projects.[22]

Better still is to have a senior manager of the principal *on site* regularly, being involved in the ongoing management of the outsourced IS project. This senior manager is not the same as the embedded liaison officer who takes part in the building of the IS project itself. Being on site during senior management meetings allows the principal to know firsthand what is happening at the project management level. The principal thereby has a real feeling for the situation, the inevitable problems that will arise, and how effective are the steps the agent might take to remedy those problems. The agent would obviously rather keep such information to itself. Being on site means the agent cannot hide it. But being on site also allows the principal to bring in its own expertise when something goes wrong, and this advice may be invaluable to the agent. This is important because outsourcing should not be treated as a zero-sum game; rather, it should be treated as either both sides gain or both sides lose.

The latter point relates to another way to alleviate moral hazard risks when outsourcing. It is about being sure the agent has a *joint interest in the success* of the project. Now, the agent has a vested interest in the project not failing. Failure, even if not the fault of the agent, means bad reputation in the market and low morale among its own people. It is better to have the project succeed, even if the agent does not make the profit it was hoping for. But from the agent's perspective there is a big difference between project success, meaning delivering on time and within quality guidelines to the satisfaction of the principal, and being a party to that success. And this is something principals do not always fully grasp. The agent, while building the software project, sees opportunities and mistakes the principal could not while planning it. As a principal you want the agent to bring these issues to your attention and to do so as early as possible. Having the agent merely fulfill the contract does not serve this purpose. It is the difference between the agent who is simply a service provider and one who has a vested interest in success beyond the payment and reputation this brings.

There are many ways the industry can create such joint interest. There is first of all the option of rewarding the agent monetarily for delivering ahead of schedule or for service beyond the requirements of the contract. This could actually be a provision in the contract. There is also the option, as in reducing adverse selection risks, of—in principle—outsourcing only to a select group of vendors (this select group would be limited to those vendors who delivered satisfactorily in the past) and possibly paying these agents above market price. Agents would rationally want to remain in this select group and would therefore go the extra mile if necessary to ensure they deliver the project satisfactorily. (See more on this issue in chapter 1.) This shifts the agent's mind-set from the short-term perspective of this one project to a longer-term relationship spanning many projects with the principal. By highlighting contradictions, missing aspects, and missed opportunities in the requirements, principals can give agents an incentive to prove their worth. And, as in addressing adverse selection risks, agents can be led to understand that part of this long-term relationship means they will have access to more profitable contracts in the future.[23] Another way to enhance agent involvement is by letting the agent take some of the credit for the success of the project. Such reputation could mean a chance to bring in future contracts with other clients. Saying an appropriate good word about the agent can go a long way toward creating a win-win situation.

A principal might also prefer agents it has extensively contracted with in the past. Taking advantage of such business familiarity not only lets the principal and agent know each other better—so each can take the necessary steps to ensure success and know what to avoid to reduce unwanted consequences—but also builds a relationship based on trust,[24] which in its own right reduces to some extent both information asymmetry and the incentive to take advantage of it.[25] Indeed, research concentrating on the principal has shown that business familiarity is a key consideration in granting contracts to agents, presumably because it reduces information asymmetry and identifies trustworthy agents,[26] and, as case studies show, it is crucial in software development outsourcing.[27] Business familiarity is of special interest as well in the context of moral hazard risks because it improves communication and mutual understanding[28] and reduces the need to rely on costly contractual controls and verification protocols,[29] such as the cost of creating and monitoring more complex and lengthy contracts.[30] Doing business with a trustworthy partner also means that each party can rely on the other to do the right thing for both sides after the contract has been signed and will not take undue opportunistic advantage of the situation.[31]

Notice that legal action is not discussed here. There is a reason for that. By the time legal action may be an option the project will long since have been over. Legal action might be nice for revenge and may result in some compensation when things go wrong, although it is doubtful if these could cover all losses, but it will not solve the problem of the project not being delivered on time. Besides, putting litigation into the relationship with the agent is bound to add a sour taste to it. And if the agent knows it may face litigation or penalties then it will raise its price to account for these extra risks it is taking.[32] Higher outsourcing price is obviously not in the interest of the principal.

Managing the Risk of Unexpected Contingencies

The risk of unexpected contingencies cannot be avoided in large IS development projects and especially in outsourced ones. The first category of such risks deals with the nature of IS. Large software projects can be so amazingly complex that it is hard for any one person to see the whole system. It has long been a maxim that one should manage such projects with a mind-set that there will always be new topics that will need to be added into the requirements after everything has been approved.[33] This is to be expected, as it is too much to expect users to see the entire picture of the system—often described in thousands of pages with all its interwoven connections within itself and to other systems—until they try it out. Based on typical empirical numbers in projects I managed, one could expect up to about half the software problem reports in a new project to be tied to the need to expand the requirements or to address topics that were left out of the original set of requirements.[34] The complexity of large software projects also means that things will unexpectedly go wrong and delay the project. In one project I took part in everything went beautifully in the initial testing phase, but the moment the project went live—and we had not tens of users but thousands of users simultaneously—the database froze. It was just not calibrated for so many transactions. As a result, to the embarrassment of senior management, project release was delayed by a day until the database expert from IBM could come on an emergency basis to deal with it. These risks are exacerbated in the case of outsourcing because the requirements typically need to be frozen once the contract has been signed and the vendor has committed its personnel to it based on cost.

Apart from those requirement and technology risks, the quick advent of technologies also adds to the risk of unexpected contingencies in the form of new game-changing technologies such as, in 2009, mobile computing and, with it, support for supervisory control and data acquisition (SCADA)[35] and Cloud computing (see chapter 1) in 2010. A company may plan its IS properly, but by the time the IS are delivered, or maybe even beforehand, the new IS may need to be adapted to support new, originally unexpected but now essential technologies.

The theoretical literature is replete with hypothetical models of how to deal with such contingencies, discussing models of renegotiation and joint ownership.[36] These models are not widely used in companies we discussed IS outsourcing with. The industry often addresses this either by signing a new contract for the changes and additions or through signing the original contract as X+Y contracting (see chapter 1). In X+Y contracting, once the contract has been signed, the original requirements are frozen as is and then developed typically on a fixed price basis (the X), while additional requirements and changes are addressed as a separate phase in the contract (the Y), usually based on time and materials. Other options include splitting large projects into a set of interrelated smaller ones.[37] Having the scope and length of each phase shorter allows companies to adjust their requirements of the next phase to unexpected contingencies. This was typical of IS project management[38] and is used in outsourcing, too.[39] In addition, there will likely be fewer unexpected contingencies when the project is shorter. It is all a matter of the KISS principle, standing for "Keep it simple, stupid!" You control your risks by avoiding complex contracting.[40] Otherwise, the way CIOs interviewed deal with this issue is through creating a trust-based relationship with the agent, just as in the case of dealing with moral hazard risks. CIOs augment the formal contractual controls with implicit informal controls as well, such as developing joint values, shared beliefs, rituals, and social connection with the agent.[41]

The Agent's Side in Agency

Agency theory deals with the theoretical aspects of contracting from the perspective of the principal. This does not mean by any stretch of the imagination, however, that the side of agent in outsourcing contracting is not crucial. Moreover, even from the principal's perspective it is important to understand the agent's side—not only because the agent is obviously a key player in this relationship and things will not work out without it but also because to properly understand the strategy and the options of the principal itself one must understand the agent. The saying, attributed in part to the Earl of Chesterfield, may claim, "He who pays the piper calls the tune,"[42] but in reality the piper in the 21st century, as perhaps opposed to the one in the 18th, can, and in the case of outsourcing often does, choose whom to play for. A more accurate saying would be "It takes two to tango," or, in this case, to make an IS outsourcing contract a success.

The underlying issue facing the agent in an agency situation involving outsourcing parallels the one of the principal, namely, information asymmetry and the risks this entails, although in the case of the agent this information asymmetry is because the principal knows more than the agent does. Although agency theory does not explicitly deal with these risks or call them adverse selection, moral hazard, or unexpected contingencies risks, the agent must still contend with a principal who knows more than it does about the business environment and the project and who has its own objectives in the relationship—objectives that are by definition almost always not the same as those of the agent. Let us examine these risks and their consequences.

Paralleling adverse selection risks, before the contract is signed the agent has only partial knowledge about what is required and what the principal really expects. The RFP may be detailed, as indeed it should be, but there is often much informal information that needs to be considered beyond what the RFP contains and beyond what the principal tells about itself. This includes internal politics, and it is typically politics and not technology that makes IS projects fail,[43] and it is typically politics that determines the nature of outsourcing relationships and their success.[44] This missing information may also relate to the technical details of the project. And so, while the agent knows a lot based on the RFP itself—as well as other information it could and should glean from the principal based on formal inquiries, publications, informal chats, other partners, its own prior work with the principal, or any other source—deciding to bid on an RFP remains a decision made with only partial knowledge. Add to this that deciding to bid is not just a matter of to bid or not to bid and the price it takes. It is also, no less importantly, a matter of what personnel to commit to the proposal. An IS RFP is not necessarily won based on price alone. Rather, the principal often reviews, in tandem with the price, who the key agent's personnel are, even to the extent of actually interviewing the key personnel the agent proposes to assign to the project. As a result, it is not necessarily the lowest bid that wins.[45]

Another equivalent of adverse selection risk is that bidding is expensive. The agent needs to invest time, meaning money, in understanding the RFP and the principal and, based on this understanding, determine the bid amount and maybe even recruit key personnel to make its bid as attractive as possible. This is a considerable investment, and there is the constant risk that someone else might win the RFP or the principal may withdraw it altogether. The agent needs to choose whom to even consider bidding for. Basically, the agent needs to know that the principal will be a "good" client. If the principal is going to be mired in internal politics, or is not committed to the project despite publishing the RFP, or is unable to guarantee that the necessary key personnel on its own side will commit enough time to the agent (something the agent should demand in the contract), or does not quite know upfront exactly what it needs, or has unfounded ideas about how simple IS projects are, or is unaware of how much it does not know about its own business, or tries to externalize (i.e., pass the responsibility on to someone else) its own IS headache, or has a myriad of other issues, then the agent is taking a higher risk when making its bid. This is the equivalent of adverse selection risk.

Of course, the more risk the agents face because of the principal, the fewer agent companies will bid on the RFP. Fewer bidding agents is bad for the principal because the best agents, being able to pick and choose whom to work for, might decide the risk is not worth the profit and so decide not to participate in the bidding. This might result in more adverse selection risk to the principal in that the leading agents, those with the key personnel the principal really needs for the project, might not take part. Moreover, those agents who will participate in the bidding are more likely to charge higher rates to compensate for this additional risk. It is imperative, therefore, for the principal to understand the risks the agents are taking and manage the agency relationship accordingly.

The moral-hazard-equivalent risks the agent is taking bear themselves out during the project itself. If the principal does not do its part and share information as it is supposed to—for example, by not providing access to key information and personnel and by inadequately testing the software before its release—then the project could be prolonged or even fail, and this might cost the agent a lot of money. Add to this the unavoidable and expected unexpected contingencies risks, which often require the active participation and support of the principal to solve, and it becomes obvious that agents need to be careful whom they agree to work for.

What Agents Do

Software vendors know these risks very well, even if they do not mask these in theoretical terminology. Many software vendors double-check each RFP they are interested in to verify that the principal will be a client they can work with. Software vendors also usually take extensive safety margins when making a bid, just to make sure that if the principal forgot something or if unexpected contingencies arise, they can still meet the deadline and deliver within budget. It is simply not worth the cost and bother and bad PR to quarrel with a client. This type of risk is exacerbated because of the nature of software: Things always go wrong and software is always more complex than initially thought. Although theoretically the agent can share these risks with the principal through ex post facto renegotiations,[46] this is not the common practice, and it is the agent who is forced to bear these risks.[47] In the 1970s and 1980s when computer glitches, "bugs," in the vernacular of the time, were still the focus of much research it was estimated that by the time the software reaches the testing phase, which is after it has already been debugged by the programmer who wrote it, there are still about 2.36 bugs for every 1 kilo line of code (KLOC) on average, depending on the type of software being developed, although this will vary based on the type of bugs.[48]

A key step agents take to address this risk is to prefer principals they have contracted with in the past. This allows the agent not only to select principals whose needs match its own skills[49] but also to know better what the principal wants and is capable of delivering.[50] Notice how this parallels principals' strategy of also preferring agents they worked with in the past.

One way this is done is by making the bid price more attractive—another reason principals want to know what risks the agent faces. Hard data on relative pricing is secret and not available, but a hint of what this might be like can be found in large-scale online software markets, such as Rentacoder.com.* In a supplement to our study of that company[51] we found compelling evidence of this two-way preference. This is shown in Figure 4.1, which shows the relative price paid for the winning bid compared with the other bids on the same tender as a function of how many previous contracts there were between the particular buyer (principal) and coder (agent). Rentacoder.com is a marketplace where buyers place tenders with descriptions of short software projects they want written and where coders then bid on these tenders. The buyers are not compelled to choose the lowest, or indeed any, bid. Once a bid is chosen the buyer pays the amount into an escrow account that is managed by Rentacoder.com. On the completion of the project to the satisfaction of the buyer, the money in the escrow account is paid to the coder. All contracts are fixed price, and there are no post hoc renegotiations. This is an international market, although most of the buyers are from the United States. Notice how after having one previous contract with the particular buyer the coders typically give a significant discount, showing their preference for buyers they have worked for before. Also interesting, this discount quickly turns into a premium, showing that buyers also value having such previous contracting and are willing to pay for it. Also interesting is how offshore coders initially give a discount compared to U.S. coders to attract buyers who are mainly in the United States. Once the buyers' concern about the coder being foreign is relieved based on experience, the offshore coders quickly raise their prices.

Choosing which RFP to bid on, applying due diligence in learning all that can be learnt about the principal ahead of time, and knowing how much of a safety margin in the pricing and scheduling to take on those RFPs the agent does bid on are steps agents take to control their risk prior to signing the contract, which is their equivalent of adverse selection risk. Addressing their equivalent of moral hazard risk is another story. Moral hazard occurs because of information asymmetry after the contract has been signed. Here the contract has been signed and the agent is now obliged to deliver, but the agent often needs the principal to share its private information and approve access to its key personnel so the agent can have access to knowledge it might need beyond that available in the RFP

---

*Rentacoder.com is now called vWorker.com.

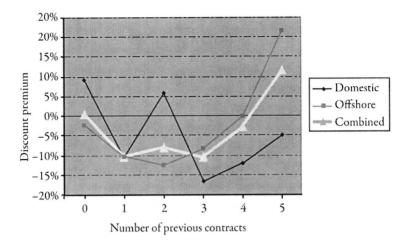

Figure 4.1. Business familiarity and discounts that agents give.

to make the outsourced project a success. It also means that the principal is willing to invest its own time and effort in the process, for example, by seriously testing the software being created and helping resolve the sometimes inevitable conflicts between what the requirements say and what the users really need. Protecting against such outcomes is not easy. Basically, an agent cannot be certain that the principal will meet all its nonfinancial obligations on the software development activities once the contract has been signed—and yet, in order to do its own share of the work properly and be paid for it, the agent depends on the principal doing precisely that, and in some cases more than the contract requires, during this process. These risks are increased because, if something goes wrong, it is the agent who is the likely candidate for blame. It is the agent who is the outsider in these projects, and it is always easier to blame the outsider.

There are many steps agents can and do take to reduce their equivalent of moral hazard risks. Managers on the agent's side, just as any other manager, need to control their risks. *The first step to control risk of any kind is to be able to define and measure it.* The same applies to agents in outsourcing contracts, too. In practical terms, this means keeping track of the progress of the project with tools such as Gantt and Pert.[52] Being able to answer the principal at any given moment as to where things stand and what comes next and how progress matches plans is crucial not only for good management but also for building trust. The same goes for constant monitoring of the numeric CSF of the project and of each milestone within it. Closely related to measuring every CSF is to *keep documentation* about everything. Principals will make mistakes and will change their minds, but if they know the agent has a record of everything then they will be more cautious about blaming and charging the agent for changes of direction during the project.

I took part in one outsourcing project where the principal complained to us, the project managers on the agent side, that there were too many glitches in the system we were delivering. This was not a malicious attack or anything. It was a standard periodic project governance meeting of the managers on the client and vendor sides to assess where things stood. Answering this would have been impossible under normal circumstances without having collected measures all along, because there are always problems so who can tell if there are too many. Fortunately, as the manager in charge, I continually collected such data, so when the question came up I could confidently relate the numbers. In this case I said up front that we had so and so many KLOCs and so and so many glitch reports, and, by the way, about half were missing specs and not our errors, and so it added up to less than the industry standard of 2.7 glitches for every KLOC. End of story. We, the agent, had answered the question and, most importantly, showed our professionalism and built trust. It also had an important side benefit. Once the principal knew we could measure their own CSF, they started relying on our numbers for their own tracking of the system. We gave them extra benefits, and they appreciated it.

Which brings us to the next thing agents can, and do, apply, which is *building trust*. Agents know things will go wrong, and agents know that as the outsider they will be the one blamed for it. That is unavoidable. But if the principal trusts you, the agent, then things will not be so bad. Suffice it to say at this stage that when the principal trusts the agent, the principal thinks more highly of the value of the relationship and the products and services it provides; and when the principal trusts the agent there is also better interfirm cooperation during outsourcing.[53] There is also better knowledge sharing,[54] and all this leads to a more long-term business relationship orientation.[55] Of course, trust is not free. You need to earn it fair and square based, for example, on keeping your word and being dependable.[56]

Trust building should be directed not only at the managers at the principal who sign off on the project but also at the principal's users. It is important to remember that *when IS projects do not succeed it may be because of technology problems, but when they fail it is most often because of people problems.* As one CIO put it: "I can make a project fail, but I can't make it succeed. For that, I need my [non-IT] business colleagues."[57] Building the trust of the users can be a crucial step toward reducing such people problems. In one outsourced project I managed from the agent's side we created and implemented a new logistics management system. Senior management at the principal loved the new system and signed off on it at the testing phase, but when we started implementing it the users who were supposed to use it vehemently opposed it. I sat with some of them at their warehouse to discuss it (note that this was at their warehouse and not in headquarters, so I was broadcasting a strong message of "I am coming to you"). Apparently, the users felt very strongly that the new IS was not their system because they were not consulted about it, and, worse, they feared the consequences of what might happen after the new IS went into operation. This was a case of us versus them, or, more precisely, white collar versus blue collar at the principal's organization. It had nothing to do with technical problems or glitches with the IS itself. Still, I heard them out. I even went beyond what I was allowed to do and let them register their problems directly with me, thereby circumventing the white collar quality assurance engineers. I made them know they were part of the process. This built their trust in me, the manager on the agent side. And it broke the us-versus-them barrier. Years afterwards studying another company I could show what happened there:[58] by being responsive an agent can create a sense of shared values and of being one team, which in turn increases the users' acceptance of the new system. This is not a unique idea. I have seen many project managers on the agent side behave so, realizing that you also need to buy the users over to your side. This is helpful because, as a manager with the agent, you want the users on the principal side to be willing to go the extra mile for you.[59]

Agency Costs

When considering IS outsourcing through the lens of agency theory it is necessary to also consider agency costs. Outsourcing vendors will sometimes claim to achieve a 50% cost reduction. On account of cheaper wages in low-labor-cost countries this may be true, but when factoring in the additional costs the principal incurs when outsourcing this number is closer to 20%.[60] Among these monitoring costs—that is, transaction costs the principal incurs to make sure the process controls are within the contractually agreed range—are the direct costs of overseeing the agent, costs of verifying quality produced by the agent, administrative costs in contracting and checking reports and ongoing meetings with the agent, and costs in dealing with contractual breaches. These extra activities are needed because the agent has its own objectives and must therefore be overseen. Of course, the agent also has its own costs in monitoring the principal, and for the same reasons. These expenses are apart from costs the principal may incur if something goes wrong, such as taking protective measures in case the agent does not deliver or bungles the work.

Other costs the principal needs to think about include *learning costs*.[61] Learning costs are the costs the principal incurs as it learns how to outsource in the first place and how to outsource with the particular agent. This is about learning what outsourcing is and not about how to manage such a relationship. These costs are much higher among principals who never outsourced their IS beforehand. Investing in this learning is essential because, as with other learning processes, outsourcing may not succeed the first time around and almost certainly the principal will make mistakes. Not only are these mistakes potentially costly, but reducing their occurrence and impact by hiring experts to coach the principal will itself add to the cost of the project. A consistent message both CIOs and practitioner books give is, do not outsource if you do not know how to. Learning costs may seem prohibitively expensive, but avoiding them is risky.

Then there are also the *resource costs*.[62] Included in this category are costs the principal will incur in employing the right people and placing them in the right positions to oversee the agency process. This includes having the right project leadership, which is not simple because the kind of manager needed to oversee the agent is not the same kind of manager needed to oversee on-site operations. It is about having a manager who knows what is needed and how to convey this, rather than a manager who knows how to do it and micromanage. It is key to have the right person in charge.[63] Also included in this category are communication costs and verification costs. Add to these the finance costs of contracting with the agent, the legal costs of writing the contract, the operational costs of actually overseeing the agent, and the cost of doing business such as writing and publishing tenders and then selecting among the bidders, and these costs too can be quite high.

Another category of costs is *bonding costs*,[64] namely, what happens if the vendor makes a mistake and how much will it cost to correct it? This category is not always fully appreciated by non-IT managers, but it is central to the way IS project managers think. This is crucial because the cost of a glitch in software, outsourced IS projects included, is not primarily in the cost it takes to correct the software. That is negligible. What really counts is the cost to correct the data that may have been corrupted or the cost of lost opportunities and fines because the software was not ready in time. Think of a large bank. If the agent made a mistake and as a result the bank paid interest at a higher rate than it should have, the bank cannot just go and correct the clients' balance sheets. That is illegal. The bank, should it decide to damage its reputation irrevocably, would need to seek permission and then run transactions to correct the data. That is the kind of risk managers in banks are really concerned about. Paying slightly above market price is not their main concern.[65] This concern is real. As Figure 4.2 shows, often the release of new software, even if it itself is correct, may cause glitches in other parts of the system, especially when adding new application to an existing system. In Figure 4.2 the period delineators separate the data into three periods. The first is right after the release of the new IS when the IS team was struggling to stabilize the new system. The second is when the system was stabilized and new features were added within the scope of the original requirements. In the third period new applications were added beyond the scope of the original topics in the requirements. The second and third periods correspond to a typical Y section in an X+Y contract (see chapter 1). Interesting to note here in regard to bonding costs is that in the second and third periods there is a much higher percentage of software problem reports that relate to problems caused by previous corrections. In other words, as the software evolved, an increasing number of changes had to be released to deal with correcting previous erroneous corrections, or to add aspects missed in previous parts of the system, so they could now accommodate the newly added applications. This is not uncommon. New releases often result in new glitches.[66]

All added in, a typical promised costs cutting of 40% made by the agent may end up more in the range of 20% on account of those costs.[67]

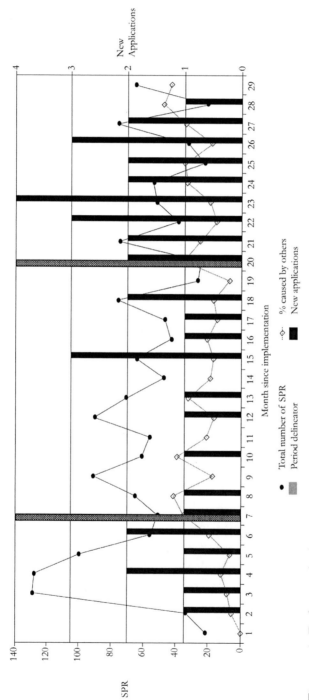

Figure 4.2. Evolution of software problem reports: a case study.

Source: Adapted from Gefen (1991).

Some industry estimates place learning and monitoring costs in the range of at least 1% to 5% of contract value.[68] In fact, in a recent CIO roundtable I co-managed, the CIOs placed the saving as low as 10% and added that it is cheaper to actually hire new people and do everything in-house than to outsource if the company plans to hold on to these personnel for the long run. When these CIOs of large companies have their choice, they would rather apply *internal outsourcing* where the projects are sent to sister organizations and offshore development centers that are part of their same organization. Industry reports support these observations: among companies who did outsource their IS, 64% have brought at least some of the outsourced IS services back in-house.[69] Interestingly, although data security is harder to achieve when outsourcing, and it is harder to manage, and vendors may lack industry-specific knowledge, still, 28% of companies sampled by *Information Week* planned to increase their business process outsourcing, 36% planned to leave it at its current rate, and only 7% planned to decrease it (27% either had not considered it or had no intention of doing it, and 2% planned to start).[70]

Another set of considerations—and the indirect costs these amount to—that principals need to consider relate to the need to make sure the agent is satisfied. If the agent is forced to bid too low, then chances are the agent might cut corners in the software development process so as not to lose money. With the agent enjoying its own information asymmetry advantage, there is little chance the principal will know of it. The agent can cut corners in many ways that may be detrimental to the principal. Some obvious examples include shifting its best personnel, and therefore more costly ones, to other projects. Other steps agents could take to cut their costs include not going through as thorough a testing as they should. Unless the principal has someone on site, there is little chance the principal would ever notice unless something went really wrong. By pinching pennies, and making the agent unhappy because of it, the principal can lose dollars. This is no mere point. According to industry sources, Osterman Research and Electric Cloud, 58% of 144 professional software developers in the United States said it was inadequate testing rather than design problems that cause problems in delivered software— and that while it only took on average 20 programmer hours to correct the bug, the lost revenue it caused amounted on average to $250,000.[71]

As many CIOs I talk to say, outsourcing is not a zero-sum game. The contracting needs to be a win-win situation, and sometimes the principal needs to be willing to pay the little extra to make that the case. Moreover, in contrast to the principal's own employees, the agent's employees owe their loyalty to the agent. If anything goes wrong or if anything is missing in the requirements these agent employees will report it to the agent. It is too much to expect them to report the problems to the principal. The principal should therefore want the agent to encourage its employees to keep their eye open for any potential problems. Unless there is a special long-term relationship with the agent, it might be too much to expect this. No less serious than keeping the agent happy is keeping its person-nel who actually do the work for the principal happy. With an attrition rate of as much as 30% in some Indian offshore software vendors,[72] it might even be too much to expect these employees to be loyal enough or care enough to report even to the agent company that employs them. Addressing these agent employee turnovers is not easy, but principals can require the agent to pay fair wages and maybe even prefer agents who have a profit-sharing scheme with their employees.

The Risk and Costs of Continual Improvements

Outsourcing IS development or maintenance presents another set of risks and the cost to address these risks. This is the risk and cost of continual improvements. It can be thought of almost as a truism in IS management that *good systems never rest on their laurels*. If the IS serve their purpose and are used, then users will identify new opportunities and request to expand the original scope of the requirements. Figure 4.3, based on the same project as is Figure 4.2, shows a case study of such a project. After the IS were released and the users started using the system, there was a continuous stream of requests for additional applications, and this was in addition to adding new features to existing applications. As these new applications were released, corrections had to be made in the existing IS to accommodate for connectivity to these new applications and to resolve bugs these new applications either revealed (now that the domain of the existing applications was expanded) or caused (e.g., by changing the pos-sible values the existing applications expected in the database and so caus-ing run-time errors when unexpected values were encountered) in the existing applications. This is to be expected in a successful IS project—but it does make planning very hard, because while IS management can schedule the release of new IS applications, it must immediately deal with the bugs the release of these new applications causes in existing applications. Bugs must be dealt with quickly because the real cost of a bug is in the damage it causes to business operations, to the data, and to missed opportunities. To demonstrate this point, industry sources estimate the cost of a bug in terms of the lost business and the damage it causes to be as high as $250,000 on average, which is by far more than the average of only about 20 work hours it takes to repair it.[73] This may be no exaggeration. In 2002 the Singapore bank DBS Bank outsourced its IT infrastructure services in Singapore and Hong Kong to IBM. In July 5, 2010, a human error by an IBM employee erroneously ran a recovery procedure on the storage system that knocked out the entire IS of the bank for 7 hours, blocking all ATM activity and affecting the bank's commercial and consumer systems.[74]

Such a need to continually modify an existing IS can present the principal with a conundrum. It is hard enough to manage continuous corrections and additions in IS that are developed and managed in-house, especially when new applications create unforeseen bugs in previous applications that must be dealt with immediately, and especially as users expect these new applications to be ready by yesterday because they do not always understand that enterprise IS are not as simple as programming a function into Excel. Doing so through outsourcing is much harder because the agent must be part of the process, too. In the case of time and materials, this means allocating more hours, which the agent may not have or the principal may not have budgeted for. In the case of fixed price contracting, this may mean a need to negotiate an addendum to the existing contract with all the delays and legal constraints involved. Moreover, it is by no means always clear whether the new bugs revealed in the previous applications were there all along but simply not found yet (in which case it is usually the responsibility of the agent to mend them) or whether these are new necessary corrections, and not bugs, to existing applications to accommodate their connection to the new applications (in which case the agent can demand additional payment). This makes the agency problem much harder to manage.

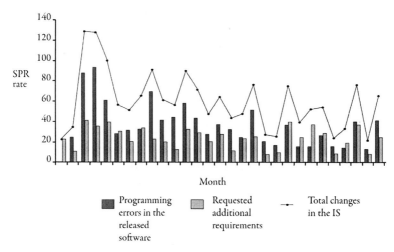

Figure 4.3. Nature of software problem reports: a case study.

Source: Adapted from Gefen (1991).

Summary of Main Point in This Chapter

In chapter 1 we introduced the outsourcing mind-set, the need to understand and control risks. In chapter 3 we then introduced the concept of
the technology imperative. In this chapter we introduced agency theory
and its expansion to deal also with the agent's side. The three ideas are
interrelated. Agency problems are exacerbated through outsourcing.
Because outsourcing is the purchase of externally produced goods or services that were previously produced internally,[75] there is an inevitable loss
of control by the outsourcing company even if the contract allows for
control and the vendor honestly submits progress and problem reports.
The key is to manage the relationship with the agent so that the risks are
known, managed, and acceptable to both principal and agent. This means
principals need to outsource constructively, concentrating on decreasing
the cost of ownership of IT, shortening time to market, increasing flexibility and innovation through IT, supporting the required IT functionality need for mergers and technology shift, achieving a strategic potential
or competence, and avoiding making the high investment on IT possible
because it is cheaper for a vendor to do so.[76] Still, although there are
many good rational reasons to outsource, there is also the irrational bandwagon effect:[77] CIOs or their managers think it is a trend and an accepted

way of doing business nowadays, and so they jump on without realizing what it entails.

In Lieu of a Boilerplate

In continuation of the structured guidelines in the previous chapter, here are more steps to follow as discussed in this chapter.

Step 4: Know your agent and treat the agent with respect.

1. Know your adverse selection and moral hazard risks.
2. Know how you may plan to deal with unforeseen contingencies during the development and implementation phases of the IS, and fully expect that if the IS are a success then there will be pressure from the users for additional functionality and modules, which will be harder to supply if the process is done through outsourcing. Additional time and materials contracts or going in the first place with X+Y contracting could be options to handle this.
3. Determine how and what to measure to keep track of your CSF.
4. Identify ways to measure and monitor the agent, including a liaison.
5. Understand what makes the agent tick and how therefore to encourage it to play your way.
6. Make sure it is a win-win situation for the agent, too.
7. Understand the pricing policy the agent is applying.
8. Calculate and monitor your costs.
9. Expect, and take steps to deal with, expanding requirements.
10. Do not believe in 40% cost savings. If it is too good to be true, then it probably is.
11. Know how to manage the relationship on more than a costs saving basis only.

CHAPTER 5

Internal Risks During Outsourcing

But first you must master their language, their dialect, proverbs and songs.
Don't trust any clerk to interpret when they come with the tale of their wrongs.
Let them know that you know what they're saying; let them feel that you know what to say.
Yes, even when you want to go hunting, hear 'em out if it takes you all day.

—Rudyard Kipling, *Norman and Saxon*[1]

Managing the Internal Risks to the Principal

Understanding and controlling risks is the key to deciding when, what, to whom, and how to outsource. Showing how critical this is, some academic research places the chance of information systems (IS) outsourcing success at only about 50% and, furthermore, highlights that despite wishful thinking IS outsourcing does not always lead to competitive advantages and cost savings.[2] In the previous chapter we examined some of these risks in view of agency theory and identified the source of risk as the infamous information asymmetry that is at the core of agency theory.[3] This agency perspective is an important aspect of what is happening in the process outside the internal premises of the principal. This chapter complements the picture by discussing the risks of what happens within the premises of the principal itself and some ways to address these risks—and recognizes that these risks, although within the internal premises of the principal, also affect how the agent conducts its bidding with the principal.

This chapter discusses the crucial importance of having the right person in charge as far as building trust and avoiding distrust are concerned, showing leadership and vision and team building, and how to achieve all of that at least partly through communicating the risks and critical success factors (CSFs) among client stakeholders to build consensus. The chapter also discusses mapping internal risks by categories into operational, financial, managerial, and other risks. The chapter then goes on to argue that risks can actually be a good thing, as long as the principal owns its own *natural risks*, namely, those risks the principal can control better than the rest of the market can.[4] Viewing these the chapter discusses how the different primary stakeholders, focusing on the chief information officer (CIO) and the chief executive officer (CEO), see things differently, and what this means when identifying and controlling for risks. This point will allow the introduction of transaction costs theory and compare its predictions to those of agency theory and trust theory. The book will discuss trust theory and its implications in greater depth in the next chapter. The chapter also discusses the importance of understanding the principal's outsourcing maturity level—whether it is outsourcing at the cost stage, resource stage, or partnership stage.

Notice how the discussion on outsourcing is following a layered pattern. The outer layer in chapters 1 through 3 dealt with the market and technology. chapter 4 then dealt with the relationship to the vendor within this market who provides the technology, and this chapter now deals with the principal itself.

Managing the Employees to Bring Outsourcing Success

The Need to Encourage Participation

The reason this view inside the principal is crucial in managing IS outsourcing is that IS development and implementation, even when done internally, are often wrought with internal resistance by users, and it is this resistance that often makes IS projects fail. This has been shown in hundreds of academic papers (some of the most noted in MIS research include the set of papers by Barki and colleagues,[5] who discuss the importance of user involvement and participation in this process, and in the work of Mumford,[6] who emphasized the importance of actively engaging the users in the decision-making process) and many industry testimonies.[7] The principal must overcome this internal resistance if the IS project is to succeed. After all, IS, no matter how useful they may seem, if they are not used by the users then they are useless. The literature, before IS outsourcing became as popular as it is, used to suggest incorporating the stakeholders into the decision-making process by sharing decision making and responsibilities with them.[8] Keeping the stakeholders and users involved in the process, apart from avoiding obvious political pitfalls,[9] allows the project management to verify how well the IS fit user needs before making changes and enables maintaining productive communications among the users and between them and the IS team.[10] Such interaction usually leads to better IS and a better fit between the IS and the organization.[11] Research shows that even when the organization mandates the use of the IS, such active user participation increases user satisfaction and project success.[12] Such *active participation* typically involves (a) granting users responsibility over estimating costs, funding, hardware and software, and managing the project, (b) enabling productive user relationships with the IS team, (c) users being involved hands-on in designing the information technology (IT) and its training programs, and (d) productive communication between the user and the IS team.[13]

And, today, when such *active participation* in the decision-making process has become impossible—as IS are used by thousands and therefore it is obviously impractical to involve all users in the process—research advocates *passive participation* by at least keeping the users informed about the IS and the decision-making process involved.[14] Keeping the users informed is crucial for a host of psychological reasons; first and foremost it shows fairness and justice, which is how people expect to be treated by others on a social level, otherwise known as *interactional justice*.[15] This type of perceived fairness on an interpersonal level refers to how those in authority interact with employees,[16] over and above the procedural rules of the organization. Interactional justice creates a sense of loyalty and increases user satisfaction[17] and positive attitude,[18] as well as reducing antisocial behavior and creating willingness to accept less favorable situations[19]—all of which could be beneficial to IS project management when it runs into inevitable problems. Moreover, when employees perceive low interactional justice they retaliate.[20] It really does not take much to create such passive participation. All it takes is for the IS team to communicate respectfully and truthfully what is happening and why and to be responsive to the users even if nothing can be done to change things. Those things alone may account for almost half the variance in the users' assessment of the new IS.[21]

An example of such business leadership during times of duress, albeit in this case in managing a company in stress that is not related to outsourcing, can be found in the case of Starbucks CEO Howard Schultz, as presented in an interview in the *Harvard Business Review*.[22] Schultz, the founder and first CEO of Starbucks, built the company into a brand name with 180,000 employees and then left the reins to others in 2000. As part of the economic crisis of 2007, there was a drastic change in people's attitude, and suddenly $5 for a cup of coffee, outstanding as the coffee may be, was regarded as excessive—and competition from lower-cost brands began picking up to capitalize on this perception. Sales plummeted and the value of the stock dropped 40%. As a result, in 2008 Schultz returned as CEO of Starbucks once again. The first thing he did to rebuild trust, realizing this was one of the things that made his company special, was to be honest with the employees by admitting the mistakes the leadership had made and honest to the clientele by not cutting quality. The second thing he did was not to break the trust and sense of family the employees had in the company. It was a matter of keeping the culture of the company the same despite the temptation to cut costs, such as by reducing health care coverage. Schultz realized that breaking this sense of trust would ruin the company. (As a parenthetical remark, the same need to create and cherish trust is crucial in IS projects, whether in-house or outsourced.[23]) He did this by calling a meeting of 10,000 store managers to New Orleans. At the meeting he reminded them of the company's values by volunteering community service to the city. And, when layoffs were unavoidable, he did not hide behind his human resources department, but rather said so directly to the employees in an open meeting, listened to their anger head on, and then apologized. You show leadership by being honest to who you are, in this case by being responsive to the employees' pain and needs and by telling them the truth, not taking the quick way out at their expense. This is again the same kind of message CIOs tell me. When you need to outsource you do your best to protect the affected employees and you explain to them what is happening and why. Trust is fragile and long term. Once it is broken, organizational culture changes, and it cannot be easily mended again.[24]

As important as active and passive participation are, it is important to realize that having the new IS developed or implemented by an agent rather than in-house only makes things harder to manage for a host of reasons, including the following: the agent is an outsider; the agent does not have as much maneuvering room in its decisions and scheduling as does an internal IT department because of contractual liabilities; the agent does not know as much as an internal IT department does about the principal and how it operates; and the contractual, rather than internal, nature of the relationship. Resolving these and other people issues within the principal's organization requires more than just addressing technical, scheduling, control, and budget issues with the agent. Nonetheless, as a matter of best practice recommendations, CIOs today apply and encourage active participation by and with the stakeholders[25] and passive participation among the users who have no real say about the budgeting and development of the IS.[26] Moreover, project management and communication become even harder when outsourcing, and yet, even though it is another company that is doing the work, the principal must continue to show leadership and vision.[27]

Perceived Contract Violation

Involving the stakeholders and users, and truthfully sharing relevant information with them, serves yet another purpose: that of reducing the feeling of being cheated. Imagine you arrive at work one morning and, without there being any previous indication about it, you learn for the first time that some of the IS services and development are being outsourced. Even if you are not part of the IT department, imagine what goes through your mind. The first thing might be uncertainty about where things might be going, but right afterwards you are concerned about betrayal, you fear for your job, and you have a profound sense of unfairness. That at least has been my experience coming into a principal organization as a project manager working for an agent. Whatever way you look at it, such emotions have a potentially negative impact on employee performance and loyalty. This type of reaction to psychological contract violation (PCV) is common and, as research in organizational settings shows, has detrimental effects on people. PCV is defined as the perception by those affected that the organization has betrayed their trust and treated them unfairly, even if the organization has not actually broken the law in doing so.[28] The result of PCV is often distrust, cynicism, and lack of motivation[29]—and, worse, this cynicism and lack of motivation also extend to other employers who had nothing to do with the employee who had been exposed to PCV.[30] This kind of atmosphere, characterized by lack of trust, results in an atmosphere of secrecy, isolation, avoidance, passivity, failure to take initiative, a sense of helplessness, doing just enough to get by, lack of involvement, and passing the blame around,[31] hardly the kind of atmosphere that is conducive to successful IS implementation.

Just how bad PCV can be was presented in the context of online markets by Pavlou and Gefen.[32] They showed that the result of PCV is a transition in people's mind-set, from initially basing interactions with others on trust (among those buyers who never experienced PCV) to basing their interaction on risk control (among those who did experience PCV). The buyers who experienced PCV tended to generalize these negative emotions to other people and circumstances that were totally unrelated to the cause of PCV in the first place. Moreover, while among those who did not experience PCV, trust-building mechanisms (such as escrows and feedback from other buyers) tended to increase trust, the very same trust mechanisms did not engender trust among those who did experience PCV—it only reduced their sense of risk.

PCV is not only a matter of statistical analyses. A look into brain activity using functional MRI (fMRI) shows the different brain activity correlates of trust and distrust perceptions. In such a study dealing with e-commerce, Dimoka[33] showed that trusting is associated with increased blood activity in the caudate nucleus, which is associated with anticipating positive rewards, and in the orbitofrontal cortex, which is associated with calculating uncertainty. In contrast, distrust was shown to be associated with the amygdala, which is associated with intense negative emotions, and the insular cortex, associated with fear of loss and risk prediction. That the amygdala is associated with distrust may explain why people will take revenge even when it is irrational to do so and they may lose even more through their actions. It is emotional, not fully rational.

Controlling PCV is crucial if an IS outsourcing project is going to be successful. This applies at least to the two primary groups of interest: the current IT team, who may rightly fear losing their positions, and to the principal's other employees, who currently receive service from their IT department and who will thereafter see a change in the nature and quality of the IS service they receive. Indeed, outsourcing could be a drastic jolt to the organization and must be managed accordingly. As discussed earlier, one Arizona CIO conveyed to me that before he outsources any IS work he makes sure to tell his IS team why he is doing so (mainly because there is too much work to be done by them alone) and how it will or will not affect them. This is correct policy. Keeping employees informed builds grassroots support for, or at least reduces grassroots objection to, the process of outsourcing. It is a matter of creating a sense of justice. The perceptions of justice are very important in organizational settings and determine employee behavior and attitudes.[34]

Create Buy-in Through Leadership

An obvious way to avoid PCV is by preparing the principal for the shock by creating grassroots support for the process. This is the same advice given to other types of drastic organizational changes, such as reengineering.[35] One way of doing so is by convincing the affected employees that they will not be negatively affected by the outsourcing process. With regard to the IS team, this can be done as the Arizona CIO did, by explaining that this was overload work anyway and would not detract from their workload or responsibilities. With regard to the other employees, if you convince them that it is their system, rather than that of senior management, and show them that the new system adds to their responsibilities and is more interesting to them than the previous IS was, then you may be able to win them over.[36] This attention to buy-in should not be underestimated. New IS and new ways of developing them typically change organizational responsibilities by taking power away from those who currently have it and are therefore wrought with internal politics that must be addressed.[37] This attention to internal politics is something any IS project leader, outsourcing or in-house, should be wary of as there is nothing managers hate more than losing the power that comes with their responsibilities. Indeed, *CIO Magazine* to this day complains that CIOs do not do enough to create buy-in, do not ask enough questions to obtain the information they need from others, and do not do enough to market the value of the IT.[38]

So, how does one go ahead and manage such buy-in? Here, too, there is no silver bullet, but there is a golden rule: Change in management requires a special kind of leader.[39] This outsourcing project leader must be able to understand the people, not just the project and the business, and to show sympathy and empathy, not with hollow words but with real caring and action. Most of all this leader must be able to build trust. When people can trust the leader they will allow him or her more credit when things go wrong, as inevitably they will, and will be more patient till the problems are solved. Building trust as a project leader is first and foremost a matter of creating and maintaining a track record people believe in.[40] To do so as an IS project leader, one must first create agreement about the overall CSFs, how to measure them, and the ranges of acceptable performance in each. Then one must establish a transparent, and therefore believable, system of measuring these CSFs. And, if things go wrong, as every now and then they most certainly will, one should not hide it or try to cover up. Covering up is not a good strategy, nor is overpromising to try to make people happy in the short term. Things come out in the end, and when people think the manager deceived them, the lost trust cannot be easily reestablished. Besides, things will always go wrong, and nobody, at least not after you show them statistics from other projects, expects you to do a perfect job every time. Openness and dependability are the key to building trust in IS projects, especially if you happen to be on the agent side.[41]

A telling example of such a change leader, in this case of an agent, is the Delhi-based HCL Technologies. In 2005 revenue was growing at an annual rate of 30%, but the company was losing market share and its competition was growing at 40% to 50% a year. The CEO realized the market was changing and that the clients wanting long-term high-quality partners to provide end-to-end services, rather than just cost cutting. As CEO Vineet Nayar tells it, his way of creating this grassroots support and buy-in is by telling the truth about where the company is right now. His policy was to openly let the employees see the risks and make these be known. He emphasized the need to recognize that what the customers care about are the people in the agent, software vendor, or organization, not its products. And so he decided to collectively build a new strategy and let the employees speak their minds. Of course this was not easy, especially given Indian culture, so Mr. Nayar decided to break the social barriers between senior management and line employees—and in doing so to take away the fear and social distance. In this case, at company meetings with employees, he decided to dance on the stage to the sound of Bollywood music and encourage the employees to join in. This rather unorthodox method did create the atmosphere he needed. Based on employee suggestions, HCL Technologies adapted a new policy of sharing financial information with the employees and letting them know where the company stood and what the challenges facing it were, as well as sharing annual plans across units. As part of this participatory policy, the company also decided to allow employees to suggest changes, to complain, and even to review their managers—quite a shift in culture, considering that previously only managers reviewed employees. The result was the creation of employee passion for the company and trust in their CEO. The board realized this and gave Mr. Nayar its full backing and support. By 2009 HCL Technologies had tripled its annual revenue, had doubled its market capitalization, was ranked India's best employer, had 55,000 employees, and while its competitors' revenues fell HCL's revenues grew by 20%—and more employees were hired.[42]

All this might sound obvious, but it is amazing how hard managers find it to live up to IBM's old maxim, which Mr. Nayar apparently inadvertently followed, that *when you go into a meeting you leave your ego outside.*

A problem that is perhaps the hardest to take care of through planning and trust management is dealing with laid-off employees and, harder still, with those who remain after others are let go because of outsourcing. There are two interrelated problems here. The first is that the knowledge these employees have is both explicit, that is, coded in a manner the agent may have access to, and implicit, that is, in their heads and not in writing anywhere, and the agent needs both these knowledge sources. But if the principal lays offs these employees, or if the remaining employees fear they may be laid off next, then it is going to be practically impossible for the agent to access this information. The second problem is that laying off employees because of outsourcing is an implicit breach of trust. This will change the whole atmosphere of the workplace among the remaining employees, as we discussed in the context of PCV. When outsourcing operations other than IS, the best advice may be to be open about it, and if you must do it then do it in one wave and let everyone know that there will be no other wave of layoffs.[43] When it concerns IS things are more complicated. One way the industry deals with such problems is by the agent hiring the affected principal employees. This, if managed with sensitivity, can alleviate both problems. The reassigned employees will not lose their jobs and so their implicit knowledge and expertise can be utilized by the agent, and the implicit breach of trust is less severe. This is actually how IBM managed its outsourcing contract with Qantas when it took over their IT services in 2009.[44] Indeed, IBM did the same in 2002 when it signed an outsourcing contract with the Singapore bank DBS Bank for S$1.2 billion for 10 years, at an expected 20% cost savings to DBS Bank, taking over 500 of the bank's IT employees—both to ensure good PR within the bank and, according to the press release, to "ensure the smooth integration of DBS Bank's staff into our operations."[45]

Managing the Project to Bring Outsourcing Success

Expecting the Unexpected

The need to plan and schedule cannot be underestimated. In chapter 4 we discussed the need to have Gantt and Pert models with reference to managing the principal–agent relationship. This need to plan milestones in detail applies as well to the internal principal doings. As the IS outsourcing project manager one must know at every moment where things stand and where the inevitable bottlenecks are. This is part of measurement and keeping track of CSFs. As a side benefit, knowing where things stand at any given moment also builds trust, as it shows that you are proficient and accurate and are not trying to hide or beautify things. Just as with the agent, the words of Peter Drucker equally apply here: "If you can't measure it, you can't manage it."[46]

But even when things seem to be going okay, you should be constantly on alert. Your mind-set should be, what am I missing, why does everything seem to be on track, where are the problems I do not see? In MBA programs we teach students to perform a SWOT analysis (strengths, weaknesses, opportunities, and threats). This is good. But it is only part of the answer even when you work as a team. There is always the risk of a team reaching consensus and then subconsciously being afraid to break the consensus, what is known in psychology as groupthink.[47] Having a harmonious team can be detrimental to business because of the complacency it may create and the atmosphere of a lack of creativity that it inspires.[48] Picking a good noble topic to fight about, doing so with fairness, and aiming at the future with a sense of purpose, and not at the past, could invigorate the organization and unleash creativity, convincing those involved of its noble purpose.[49] Adding some no-people, as opposed to yes-men, is one way to actively encourage some criticism, which is good because it counters groupthink. In identifying these problems, and there are always things you do not see, it is imperative to rely on others, both others in your outsourcing team and others among the users—and you cannot rely on these others to keep you informed unless you can build an atmosphere of trust and long-term relationships. Here too, earning the trust of others is the key to success. Regardless of how well you plan and how well you then monitor the plan, there is a chance of turmoil in the IS outsourcing process. You should plan how to deal with such turmoil. Trust is an asset in doing so.

Back to Agent Again

As the case of IBM hiring Qantas employees when it signed the outsourcing contract[50] shows, the way the principal manages the internal transition that comes with IS outsourcing is of paramount importance to the agent, too. Obviously the agent needs these principal employees to be cooperative and to share their implicit knowledge and to have good intentions, but also—just as the principal should do when choosing the agent—the agent should do its own risk assessments about the principal before deciding whether to take on this tender and what price tag to attach to it. We discussed aspects of this in chapter 4 in the context of agency relationships. The more internal turmoil the agent expects, the bigger the safety margins it will have to take on its costs and scheduling, and the more and better experts it will have to assign to the project— all this translates to a higher price tag to the principal, and in extreme cases the situation may be so bad that only desperate agents might bid. Basically, agents do their homework in choosing whom to contract with and on what terms. Preparing the principal organization before outsourcing is therefore imperative in attracting the kind of agents the principal wants and in reducing their bid price. In reengineering, taking the passive position of "do it for me" is one of the biggest mistakes a principal can make.[51] The same applies to IS outsourcing. The principal may rely on the agent regarding the IS part, although even here only with caution, but must know how to handle its own employees. Abdicating responsibility is not an option in IS management.[52]

Managing the IS Part

A key aspect of preparing the principal for outsourcing, apart from dealing with the employee side, is knowing how to manage IS projects. Regardless of whether these projects are done in-house or outsourced, IS management needs to show leadership and be an integral part of the organization, linked to its strategy, and based on a long-term perspective that, as the nervous system of the organization, integrates everything in the organization into one system.[53] Summarizing some of the best practices used in the industry in the context of IS management, not necessarily outsourced IS, Matta and Ashkenas[54] suggest that IS projects are often too complex and their risks are not always addressed properly. These risks amount to several major kinds. Among them are *execution* risks, which are typically addressed adequately; *white space* risks, which deal with requirements left out and which remain a serious problem; and *integration* risks, which are the risks involved in putting all the pieces together, and this too is a problem. To deal with these problems Matta and Ashkenas suggest splitting projects into smaller "rapid results initiatives" projects. This, by the way, is common practice also in companies we studied.[55] Indeed, research shows that small algorithms are much less likely to have bugs.[56] There are hardly any bugs when the application has less than 1,000 lines of code or when the application is a simple report as opposed to a complex update algorithm.[57]

This strategy of splitting large projects into small steps and dealing first with the low-hanging fruit is a great way to create buy-in among the employees and stakeholders. Nothing succeeds like quick success. In contrast, large multiyear projects, which are much harder to manage even when successful, do not create as much PR because of the large time lapse between initiation and delivery (during which time the stakeholders may have forgotten the original requirements or been moved to other positions with their replacements not knowing as much about the project or being as enthusiastic about it—or the market needs may well have changed so much that the original project is already outdated). Reflecting this short-project emphasis, many IS outsourcing projects today are at most 12 months long.[58]

And so, suggest Matta and Ashkenas,[59] IS project management strategy, and by extension this applies to the IS outsourcing context, too, should be to identify small problems, create buy-in, identify miss-ing specs, and then shift the responsibility from senior managers to the development team. The characteristics of such projects should be results oriented, quick, and involve vertical cross-functional projects involving several organizational units. Coming in and delivering quickly while involving all the affected parties is the key here. There is also the issue that success breeds success, and so when IS projects are successful employees and other stakeholders start believing in the change and in the new IS, and obviously the opposite is true when things fail.

What IS to Outsource

The internal risks the principal faces relate not only to managing employ-ees and the process, but also to deciding what parts of the IS to out-source. As not all IS are borne alike, it is crucial to know as part of a detailed and thought-out plan what IS to outsource and why and how to do so. The question, then, is what IS should a company consider to outsource. One could follow the advice typically given in non-IS opera-tions to keep *core competencies* in-house while externalizing (i.e., let some-one else do it) other operations. Likewise, outsource operations where the principal shows relative incompetence. Thus, it makes sense for a com-pany such as IBM to buy enterprise resource planning (ERP) systems from SAP because ERPs are not a core expertise of IBM and not where it makes its money, but not to outsource the development of key com-ponents of its DB2 database to Oracle because its database is a key soft-ware product IBM sells. Or, in the case of a bank, outsourcing its payroll on the Cloud through software as a service (SaaS) might be an option because it is standardized and there is nothing special about how a bank pays its employees. However, outsourcing the storing of its customer data through infrastructure as a service (IaaS) would not be something the bank would consider outsourcing on the Cloud because privacy of infor-mation is a key aspect of the service a bank sells. Indeed, not surprisingly, this kind of strategy is what CIOs talk about in roundtables.[60]

A variant on this approach, based again on risk management, is to acquire those risks your company has a strategic advantage in holding and outsource the others. This approach was suggested by Buehler,[61] in the context of financial markets, although its insight applies to IS outsourcing, too. Buehler and colleagues suggest as follows: Take advantage of those risks your company can handle better than other companies can. Accordingly, organizations should own those risks they can manage best, which are called *natural risks,* and outsource those risks they cannot manage better than other companies can. Doing so should save on operating costs by letting other companies with better economies of scale and specific capability handle those topics that are not natural risks. The agents in this case might also face less risk than the principal would. The result, claim Buehler and colleagues, should be higher returns on equity. Applying such an approach to outsourcing is apparently precisely why CIOs outsource, at least when they outsource the maintenance of their legacy IS so they can free their long-time employees who are experts on the organization to work on new projects.[62] In taking this approach Buehler and colleagues suggest this process: (a) Understand your company's major risks, (b) decide which of these are natural risks, (c) decide on your company's risk appetite, (d) make risk an integral part of decision making, and (e) align the company around risk management. Notice the conceptual parallels with the diffusion of innovation model[63] discussed in chapter 3. Of course, things are never as easy as they seem.

Managing the Internal Risks to Bring Outsourcing Success

In deciding what risks to own, companies must first map their risks. This is no easy task because different stakeholders in the organization will have different views of the CSFs and of how to measure them. A convenient classification of these risks as they apply to outsourcing is operational, financial, and managerial risks. *Operational risks* are risks that are related to the delivery of the service or the product. Outsourcing may externalize some aspects of these operational risks, albeit at the additional cost and risk of less control, but the risk remains. A manager at one of the leading pharmaceutical companies told me of a case his company encountered when they offshored the production of one of the ingredients they were going to use in the manufacture of one of their batches, only to discover that the agent had not followed appropriate quality control and so the whole batch had to be destroyed in accordance with FDA regulations. The company saved on pennies but paid in pounds. Operational risks are very high in IS development. We already mentioned the 30% failure rate of in-house IS projects[64] and the estimate by Gartner that IS outsourcing projects fail in around 50% of cases.[65] Other market reviews claim that while 70% of companies planned to cut costs through IS outsourcing, 37% actually ended up paying more; and while 57% of companies hoped for better quality through IS outsourcing, 31% actually complained that the vendor became complacent.[66] Indeed, underperformance, in 59% of the cases, and cost overruns, at 15%,[67] do suggest that operational risks are high. *Financial risks* are risks concerning costs. It is about paying too much but also about risks like, Will the agent still be around next year, and How much will it cost to recover if the agent fails? These risks are not the focus of this book, but they are and have been a major concern for years.[68] *Managerial risks* in this context deal with managing the people and the project involved in the process. These also include risks in overseeing the service or production of the outsourced IS. There are other types of risk, including legal risks and PR, but those are not the topic of this book.

Consider Additional IS Project Management Risks

The list of risks discussed above is obviously only a partial one and will vary, depending on the specifics of the project and organization. Some additional risks IS managers may want to consider while mapping their risks are, Will there really be increased workforce flexibility as a result of outsourcing to an agent? After all, the agent has its own liabilities and constraints, and while it may be better able to take advantage of its economies of scale and natural risks better than the principal, these are not unlimited. And, in the long run, it may actually work out to be more expensive to hire an agent than to hire people to do the same work in-house, as indeed many CIOs mentioned to us.[69]

Then there is the issue that outsourcing is not about abdicating responsibilities. The IS manager at the principal site must still make contingency plans to deal with cases of agent failure to deliver on time and within quality or to deal with cases where the agent cannot respond fast enough. Taking on an agent may shift developmental risk to the agent and possibly reduce financial risk, but ultimately if the agent cannot deliver then it will be the IS manager at the principal site who will have to somehow work things out. And having the IS work done by an agent makes preparing for such eventualities so much harder because the IS managers at the principal site do not have their fingers on the pulse the same way they would if the development was done in-house. Besides, the IS managers at the principal have only limited power to cajole the employees of the agent to go the extra mile when necessary as these employees owe their loyalty to, and are paid by, the agent, which translates to a more limited ability to respond quickly to unexpected changes.

Then there is the issue of planning. IS projects are notorious for missing things in the requirements specification. We already compared IS projects with jigsaw puzzles where one does not know if a piece is missing or is not cut properly until almost all the pieces are in place. With this analogy in mind, it may be too much to expect managers, or even the systems analysts who work with them, to elicit the detailed requirements, to see the whole picture. Now, when IS projects are developed in-house there is some flexibility to go back and add or correct aspects to the requirements. This is much harder in the case of outsourcing because in that context any major change typically requires another contract. So IS managers at the principal must continually ask themselves if all the aspects of the required software or service have been listed, and how much it will cost to add those we missed. Closely related to this is the question of whether there are hidden costs and if we have correctly accounted for the cost of checking after the agent. When these hidden costs and verifying after the agent are included the expected savings may not be there. For example, IS outsourcing agents may promise a 40% cost reduction and show the numbers to support this based on their economies of scale and experience, but when the transaction costs of managing the contract and the relationship with the agent are included, these percentages may become much lower. Some estimates put these additional transaction costs alone at 5% to 10% of the total contract cost in some types of outsourcing.[70]

And there is the question of when the project is completed, will the agent become complacent once it has the principal hooked, as reported by some industry reports,[71] and will this have an effect on the rigidity of the service? Likewise, should the agent underperform, does the principal know how to measure this, and does it have an exit plan to replace the agent? This is no mere issue. Good IS never rest on their laurels. Once an IS has proven itself, users will request new functionality to support the new opportunities the new IS have created. And often these users do not understand that complex IS are not as simple as Excel and Word so these additions cannot be ready by yesterday. See Figure 4.2 for an example of how many such new requests one can expect. And, of course, the principal has to pay the agent for these additions and changes.

There are no publicly available data on what financial safety margins principals take to address these additional risks, but on the agent side I can testify from my own experience that when we placed a bid on a tender, we the project managers on the agent side would take as much as a 300% safety margin on time estimates so we could be reasonably assured we had enough leeway to address unexpected contingencies with the requirements, technology, and our own workforce. These numbers were seldom an exaggeration.

Example of Managing Internal Risks

Imagine you are the IT director in a large bank. The Federal Reserve has issued new regulations, and your bank has 6 months to comply. These new regulations translate to changes in the IS you are in charge of and will require extensive new software development. You know what needs to be done, or at least you think you do, but do not have the personnel to do it. In consultation with the CFO and the chief operations officer (COO) you are told to outsource. This is not your choice. They want to control cost and delivery time risks. You would rather control your development risks and keep it in-house or hire experts on an hourly basis to help out. You do not want to lose control but have no choice.

At this stage the risks you and the bank face are several. There are operational risks that the outsourcing process will not work as planned and risks that the software that will be developed might not be ready on time or not meet the specs. Then, there are financial risks that the agent might be paid too much or that the contracting costs will be higher than budgeted. There is also the ever-present financial risk that the software might malfunction and corrupt the data, which is a legal nightmare. Such incidents of corrupted data explain why some industry reports put the cost of a bug at an average of only 20 programmer hours to correct, but at an average revenue cost of $250,000.[72] And there are managerial risks in managing the relationship with the vendor and with the employees within the bank and that its implementation may not be smooth. You are able to define measurable CSFs for each of these broad categories of risks together with your tolerance levels for each. You can even control some of these risks by breaking up the project into small parts, as Matta and Ashkenas suggest.[73] You also have the IS development process cross-sectional and integrative of all the bank departments involved to make sure everything is in sync with the bank's strategy and culture, as Feld and Stoddard suggest.[74] Moreover, this new software module development and its outsourcing are going to be managed as part of a long-term disciplined IS strategy, also as Feld and Stoddard suggest.[75]

Given the high operational risks, all involved, including the CFO, agree that the tender will be published only to a limited number of software agents. These are the agents the bank had worked with extensively in the past and who all got flying colors in the postproject evaluations your team did after each outsourcing project they took part in. Postproject evaluations and the analysis of what was done correctly and what could have been improved are an integral part of good IS project management, even when it is not outsourced. Limiting the tender to only trusted agents is standard practice; except in special circumstances only trusted agents are considered when risk is high, certainly on this type of project. You also all agree that each contending agent will have to agree to let the bank interview and choose its key personnel on the project, and, a priori, have veto over who among those agent personnel does what in the project. Likewise, the CFO, COO, and you agree that there will be no subcontracting, so the bank will have more control over the process. All these are common industry practices, and the bank, as a very big client, can demand it. You know the agents will agree, especially when they realize how high the stakes are.

So far so good, except that when it comes to the details, things become more complex. As the truism says, "Where you stand depends on where you sit." Or, to be precise, how you rank the conflicting CSFs and their critical values depends on the organizational responsibility you have within the bank. Controlling the financial risks the CFO is most concerned about, the question might be, Does the bank prefer agent 1 who is very good and costs 5% less than the average bid you received on this tender? Or, does the bank prefer agent 2 who can deliver the software possibly faster and with better quality controls and less lines of code (there is a very high correlation between the number of lines of code and the number of bugs) but costs 5% more than the average? Five percent extra costs may be unjustifiable extra costs to the CFO, but this agent is less risky for the IS project manager who trusts this agent more. Or, perhaps agent 3 should be chosen, because agent 3, whose costs are about average, has an excellent reputation within your bank based on its ability to be responsive and helpful to the users, which you know is going to be a crucial managerial risk here. Or perhaps agent 4, who is suggesting a 50% discount because it has done this same type of project before and is proposing a SaaS solution.

The first thing you do is to map the obvious risks. The main risks are (a) the bank not complying with the new regulation, (b) not being on time, or (c) not implementing the software correctly because the users do not understand it. Any of these will amount to such a hefty fine that saving 5% on contract price will be meaningless. These are the real CSFs. It is not about saving costs. Then, there are longer-term risks: (d) not being able to provide proper maintenance to the software because it is not written and documented properly, (e) choosing a vendor who might go out of business before the software is ready or whose personnel turnover is such that its implicit knowledge about the project will be compromised, or (f) having an agent who may not honor the confidentiality forms it signed. Here, too, saving 5% on the contract is not your CSF. For each of these risks you assign a measure of success and determine your tolerance levels around it. Complying with regulations must be 100% and there cannot be any tolerance for error as neither you nor the bank can afford to have the Federal Reserve question your performance. As to being on time, you have 6 months, so you plan to have the software delivered within 4 months, which is your measure of success on this CSF, so you can start testing it. Your tolerance level here might be a week, because even if the agent delivers a week after the milestone requires it, you can still make up for it with the safety margin you deliberately took when you said 4 months. There are implementation risks, as well. You plan to have the IS delivered at least 2 months in advance so you can run extensive training. Here, too, you can have some tolerance on this delivery date. As to maintenance, there is some tolerance on quality, if only because you cannot fully measure it, but you will insist on having the software checked module by module by your most pedantic testers and refuse to accept it if it is not perfect. As to (e) and (f), there is no tolerance: if you are not certain about the agent then there is no deal with it.

You as the IS leader know you must now convince the CFO to come on board with your choice. The politics require it. You also know that saving 5% as important as it is, and rightly so, to the CFO, is not the only key issue. What really counts to you as the IS manager are software quality and preferably first, being on schedule with it, and second, smooth implementation. So you choose the more expensive agent 2, and perhaps subcontract part of the implementation to agent 3. Cost savings is not the key CSF you are concerned about. Indeed, CIOs emphasize in talks that, at least when it is up to them, it is not the cheapest bid that wins. As to agent 4, well, this agent is out of the question because it is bank policy to own the software outright. The IS are the equivalent of the nervous system, so they are owned in-house, period. What you might do in this case is to create a short list of the agents, in this case only agents 2 and 3, arguing that you as the IS expert have the prerogative, responsibility, and knowledge to make sure only appropriate agents for this specific project are considered. Thereafter, let the CFO choose.

Within this process, the IS manager mapped the risks, probably including many more than discussed here, and assigned to each risk the degree of damage it might cause and likelihood of this happening. Additionally, the IS manager mapped how these risks relate to company-owned risks. In this case the natural risks of the bank are investment in such software, which is why agent 4 was not considered.

The Outsourcing Maturity Level Model

In the previous chapters we discussed outsourcing in the context of companies trying to cut costs combined with the technology imperative to outsource and the user imperative. In a nutshell, the technology imperative discussed in chapter 3 recognizes that technology today is such that no one company can master it all, especially as technology develops and changes so quickly that it is hard to prepare, plan, and develop the expertise in-house. Because of this technology imperative companies need to acquire this expertise from the outside. Indeed, even technology leaders such as IBM have been acquiring new expertise through other companies. The announcement in July 2009 that IBM is acquiring SPSS, a company that provides one of the leading statistical analyses software packages, to improve its data-warehousing capabilities is an example of this trend. This acquisition of expertise outside the company is aided by technology becoming more standard and interconnected, and so with less proprietary technology. These trends of acquiring capabilities from outside the company combined with these technologies being available thanks to the transition in the marketplace from a silo-oriented market to a segmented market (see Figure 3.2), and aided by an increased user imperative to purchase ready-made standardized IS solutions rather than develop proprietary ones, marks a shift in the "maturity" of marketplace.

IS outsourcing marketplaces go through three stages of maturity: cost stage, resource stage, and partnership stage.[76] In the *cost stage* companies outsource because it is cheaper to outsource than to do the same activity or process in-house. It is a question of transaction costs: since the vendor has economies of scale and scope, it is cheaper to contract the vendor. Outsourcing may also cut costs by allowing the client to hire fewer employees or let off its relatively expensive employees. This type of outsourcing deals mainly with standardized processes and products. This is the world Carr[77] is talking about when he recommends treating IS as a utility. The contract in this case is legally binding with a detailed service-level agreement (SLA), explicit rights and duties of each party, with codified responsibilities and policies, and usually with penalties should the agent not deliver on time or within quality CSF measures. The relationship between the client and the vendor is an agency relationship of the kind discussed in chapter 4, with an implied competition between the client who is the principal and the vendor who is the agent. This is the lowest level of outsourcing maturity.[78] The key objective here is cutting costs with a well-defined service in a standardized market. It is not about acquiring capabilities.

The next stage in outsourcing maturity is the *resource stage*. At this stage the client also has access to the vendor's resources, both tangible, such as licenses, and intangible, such as knowledge. The key objective here is acquiring knowledge and capabilities. This maturity stage is the result of the technology imperative and the shift in the IT market from a silo-oriented market to a segmented one. The business relationship at this stage is still legally binding, still based on formal relationships and explicit SLA, and still has an agency aspect to it as the principal and agent remain separate companies, although the competition between them is weaker.[79]

The highest stage in the maturity model is the partnership stage. In the *partnership stage* the emphasis is on intangibles: It is about trust, understanding, cooperation, shared goals and values, regular communications, and interpersonal relationships. It is about an alliance-bound relationship that aims at mutual benefit. This is not an agency relationship because the parties have compatible goals.[80] This is how IBM describes it relationship with SPSS. It is a matter of mutual benefits geared toward a merger. In this case one of the objectives, at least according to the newsletter they released, is that "IBM is expanding its focus on business analytics technology and services to meet growing client needs to cut costs, reduce risk, and increase profitability through predictive analytics capabilities, which include advanced data capture, data mining and statistical analysis."[81] Acquiring this type of relationship should allow IBM quick access to the top-notch statistical analysis tools and experts that SPSS has. Even in business relationships where one company does not form an alliance or buy the other this kind of relationship can exist; for example, when both client and vendor want to showcase the project they are currently working on to show how good they are.

Maturity has serious implications for what companies outsource there IS and why. At the cost stage the objective is cost minimization and operational efficiency. At the resource stage it is about client productivity and technology innovation. At the partnership stage, in contrast, it is about business benefits and mutual goals. The contractual considerations are also different. At the cost stage the emphasis is on the SLA, which details the exact requirements the client needs and the exact details of the software or service being delivered. Accordingly, the exact obligations of the client and the vendor are specified in minute detail, including pricing (sometimes even at the level of the cost of each activity), warranties, liabilities of both sides (who owns the assets and how they will be transferred from the vendor to the client), and, importantly, the dispute resolution mechanism. The same details might apply at the resource stage, too, but the objective is more on actual project success than on deliverables. The partnership stage also details these, but the objective here is also mutual profits. These implications directly affect how the principal monitors and tries to control the agent. At the cost stage it is about controlling either the behavior of the agent in time and materials or the outcome in fixed price contracting. The cost stage is about structured relationships with an emphasis on measurement of detailed service quality. As the maturity level goes up to the resource stage, the relationship becomes less structured and has more of an emphasis on overall service quality. At the partnership stage the relationship is even less structured and the emphasis is on the long-term impact.[82]

As an example of the cost stage, think of buying PCs. This is a standard product with standard service and known quality controls. Since the SLA can be defined exactly, the issue at stake is cost. Installing an ERP, in contract, might fit better into the resource stage. Here, the vendor knows so much more than the client that defining an SLA might actually be detrimental to the latter. The client's objective is to tap in to the vendor's knowledge to help define what exactly it needs. Because the client does not know enough to define the SLA in sufficient detail, it does not know how to compare vendors, and therefore the cost of the service, although always important, is of lesser importance than in the cost stage. The partnership stage is different. Here companies cooperate to develop together. The cooperation between Dell and Intel in building new PC systems, where both have a shared interest in the mutual success of their PCs and chips, respectively, is an example of this. This, of course, requires knowing the marketplace.

The CIO Versus CEO Views

The maturity model highlights an important reality check about organizations: There are many stakeholders in the outsourcing decision and each has its own CSF and objectives. Three of the major players in IS outsourcing decisions are the CIO, the CFO, and the COO. The CEO may also become involved if it is a strategic decision. The role of the CFO in smaller projects may be managed by accounts payable, that of the CIO by the IS project leader, and that of the COO by the operations manager whose operations are being affected by the new IS being acquired through outsourcing, or by the consequences of outsourcing the IS that had up to now been managed in-house.

The CFO (as the title implies) is legally responsible for the financial aspects of the company, which in the case of outsourcing includes cost control and where necessary saving money. The CFO and the accounts payable department that reports to the CFO are also responsible for obeying the accounting regulations, which in some cases may preclude showing preferential behavior toward agents the COO and the CIO would really rather work with. The key concerns the CFO has in outsourcing is the question of cost, financial control such as making sure the agent in a time and materials contract is not overpaid, and that the accounting and contracting regulations are followed to the letter. The CFO is aware of the operational risks that concern the COO, and the quality of the software and its related service that perturbs the CIO, but those valid risks are not the three or four CSFs that concern the CFO the most. The CFO and accounts payable would probably be late majority managers. The CFO and accounts payable are always key decision makers in major outsourcing decisions because there is always an element of money and payments involved in outsourcing. Basically, the CFO or accounts payable must approve and secure the funding if the outsourcing project is to ever begin. The mind-set of the CFO and accounts payable would fit into the costs savings portion of the outsourcing maturity model.

The COO, on the other hand, is worried about smooth ongoing operations. The IS to these managers are merely tools that make things happen. To these managers, IS are a necessity, almost like having electricity. And, like any other utility, the IS are expected to work flawlessly. That IS do not always behave so is a constant agitation to these managers. These managers may be willing in their own domain to take the risk of trying new technologies and other managerial ideas if they think these may help do the work they are responsible for better and certainly if these technologies and ideas have been shown to work elsewhere. This makes them early or late majority managers. But, when it comes to IS, they either are unfamiliar with the implications of the IS or do not care, and so these managers would rather not try anything new that they do not understand about the IS they are using. To them, any changes in the IS are unnecessary risks. Treating IS as a utility, these managers want solutions from IS; they are not concerned about the IS issues themselves.[83] They are not happy to take risks for the sake of a new IS they do not understand, they are not responsible for, and, at worse, that might mess up the operations they are responsible for. To these managers, changes in the IS are not welcome. Whether changes in the IS came through development in-house or through outsourcing, they mean more operational risk with no additional rewards. Again, it is not that the COO or operations manager is unaware of the risks that most concern the CFO or the CIO, it is just that they are faced with enough risks of their own with time to market, production quality, reducing operational risks, and so on. CFO and CIO risks take second place, and besides, the CFO and CIO can, and demand to, handle their own headaches and risks. These managers do not hold any easily identifiable place on the outsourcing maturity model.

The CIO and IS project managers have different outlooks. Their concerns are about the quality of the IS, its schedules, and its implementation. Also to these managers costs are always important, and so they understand the position of the CFO, and they are, or should be, fully aware of the consequences on operations if the IS they are outsourcing malfunctions in some way, and so they also understand the position of the COO. But their main concern and organizational responsibility is a matter of the software and its services. Because the CSFs of these managers are the software and its delivery, to them outsourcing also has a strong element of obtaining expertise. These managers are likely to focus on the cost savings if the outsourcing is done with the objective of releasing their own IS personnel from maintenance work so they can develop new systems. Alternatively, if these managers are outsourcing because of the technology imperative, then they are most likely to be at the resource stage of the outsourcing maturity model.

The other possible key player, the board of directors, is not likely to be part of the detailed decision-making process in IS outsourcing. The board, because of all the other responsibilities thrown at them by the regulating authorities, do not have the time to deal with CIO-level decisions. Their hands are too filled to overflowing with oversight of the CEO and CFO to spend time on the "technical" issues that concern CIOs.

Transaction Costs Economics and Outsourcing

An alternative way of looking at IS outsourcing is through the lens of the theory of transaction costs economics.[84] This theory is a convenient way to understand the view of the CFO. In a nutshell, according to this theory companies externalize work, that is, they contract with other companies or buy what they need on the market instead of making it in-house, because their hierarchies and decision-making process make it more costly and less efficient to manufacture in-house than to purchase on the market. Applying this theory to outsourcing, companies outsource because it is cheaper for them to buy the IS services and products through an agent on the market than to develop them in-house. Companies nonetheless exist, according to this theory, because there are always transaction costs in markets. These transaction costs are associated with finding the right price, identifying suppliers, bid process, quality assurance, contracting, verifying, and so on. All these transaction costs add up to making the market price of some products and services more expensive than manufacturing in-house. And so when it is cheaper to conduct business within the company rather than in the market, business stays within the company; this happens because of asset specificity. Asset specificity means that an asset or an expertise is worth more in one context than in another because it is specific to that context.

For example, think of an electric utility company that generates electricity by burning coal. When there are many coal mines around, then it is cheaper for the utility to buy coal on the open market. But when there is only one coal mine nearby then it may be cheaper for the utility to own this one mine.[85] When there are many mines, market forces will force the price down so that only those few really efficient mines remain in the market. Competition would thus probably make it cheaper to buy coal on the market than to manage the mine with all the additional costs of the hierarchies and decision making at the utility. But when there is only one mine, then the transaction costs of running a market with only one mine and one utility company would likely be higher than the hierarchies and decision-making costs at the utility if it owned the mine. Therefore, since it would be cheaper overall to own the one mine, the utility company would be wise to own it in this case.

There are many such types of asset specificity says Williamson. There is site specificity, such as in oil drilling; physical asset specificity, such as the U.S. Air Force only having F-22s; human asset specificity, such as companies having employees with very specialized human skills; and dedicated assets, such as investment in a machine that cannot be easily applied to other purposes. To this list Malone and Laubacher[86] add time specificity, such as a human heart for a heart transplant that is only valuable for a limited time. As a rule, low-specificity assets are better managed by the market, while high-specificity assets are better managed in-house.

A low-specificity asset can be transferred easily to another transaction. A PC is such a low-specificity asset. It can be used for many purposes by many companies in many places. It is easy to change the use of a PC, and its capabilities are important to almost any company regardless of what it does. A company does not have any advantage in owning a specific PC. They are standard. A PC is a low-specificity asset. With low-specificity assets, it is cheaper to buy them on the market or rent them than it is to have a special contract from one vendor to provide them or to manufacture them in-house. Companies use least-cost governance to manage these assets. Buy the cheapest model that still addresses the needs would be the guideline here. The same applies to the software market. Knowing C++ is a low-specificity asset. Many programmers know C++, and their knowledge is applicable to many projects and companies. This knowledge is to some degree interchangeable among programmers, and a company has no advantage in holding one C++ programmer over another (unless of course other factors are brought into consideration). In contrast, high-specificity assets are more valuable in one context or transaction than in another. For example, an expert on a specific software algorithm or database the company owns is a high-specificity asset. This expert is worth a lot to this company, but the expert's knowledge may be worth little elsewhere. In this case, companies retain these high-specificity assets in-house and use internal governance to prevent unwanted lock-ins.[87]

Applying this theory to the Cloud may suggest that Cloud computing will become popular with low-specificity assets, such as e-mail and disk memory, but less so with more specific custom-tailored services. Risk is the key. Indeed, industry reports about the Cloud show it is not the panacea some claimed it to be.[88] And this is precisely the reason why IS outsourcing projects are not the same as other projects. It is not only a matter of budget, which is what the CFO cares about; nor is it a matter of doing the job properly, which is what the COO cares about. It is first of all a matter of high-specificity assets, and therefore quality control is crucial, especially in the case of software. In the case of software it is inevitable that there will be problems and that at least to some extent a company will lose control when it outsources. With the cost of a problem measured realistically in terms of the damage it causes and the lost opportunities it results in, rather than the standard transaction cost economics (TCE) measures of alternative costs, the CIO will see things differently.

In Lieu of a Boilerplate

Things at this stage are so complex there is no "in lieu of a boilerplate."

Summary of Main Point in This Chapter

Successful outsourcing requires having the right person in charge, and what this person must do is map the risks so they can be controlled. Part of controlling these risks is about managing the transition within the company. It is imperative to manage the transition by building trust and understanding and communicating the risks and CSFs among client stakeholders. These risks will relate to operational, financial, and managerial issues, as well as many others we have not discussed in this chapter. One way of choosing which risks your company should own and which it should outsource is to retain the *natural risks*, those risks your company can control better than the rest of the market can. It is also imperative to understand the outsourcing maturity level of the company and whether it is in the cost stage, resource stage, or partnership stage. Regardless of where it stands, though, the IS outsourcing manager should realize that different stakeholders have different risks and therefore different CSFs. One convenient way of understanding the CFO side of things is through TCE, where the bottom line is always the bottom line. This perspective contrasts with the agency perspective of the CIO or IT manager.

CHAPTER 6

Managing Risks in Interacting With the Agent

Appear with your wife and the children at their weddings and funerals and feasts.
Be polite but not friendly to Bishops; be good to all poor parish priests.
Say "we," "us" and "ours" when you're talking, instead of "you fellows" and "I."
Don't ride over seeds; keep your temper; and never you tell 'em a lie!

—Rudyard Kipling, *Norman and Saxon*[1]

Perspective

To fully understand information systems (IS) outsourcing, it is imperative to understand the agent and how to manage the relationship with the agent, so that all parties involved, including the agent, may gain from the relationship, or at least not lose anything from it. Understanding the agent is another facet of controlling risks. Recall that risk is any variation beyond the predefined tolerance levels of the expected measured values of any of the critical success factors (CSFs). This variation relates to both tangible CSF measures—such as price, costs, savings, time to market, schedule, quality, outcome measures—and, most important, to the intangible and therefore harder to measure and predefine but still crucial CSF measures such as satisfying internal politics, stakeholders, and invested interests and overcoming users' resistance to change, and so on. Involving the agent as a stakeholder in the process is partly what this chapter is about. It takes two, the principal and the agent, to tango, but the two must be attuned to each other if it is going to work. Indeed, as Feld and Stoddard[2] put it, "the 'gears' become even more critical when you bring outsourcing and offshoring into the picture, because management complexity rises. You can't abdicate the leadership and vision for these critical functions."

Put into context, this chapter is about risks in the contracting process and mitigating these risks through the request for proposal (RFP) process and the contract. Both the RFP and the contract lay the land for the tango relationship between the principal and the agent and for the risks in the way the principal and the agent interact with each other. Managing these risks requires both the principal and the agent to be cognizant of them, and both individually and in tandem need to take steps to measure and then control these risks. These risks are apart from the adverse selection risks in choosing the right agent, and then the moral hazard risks once the chosen agent starts working on the project, combined with the inevitable unexpected contingencies that arise because of the complexity of the IS and the ferociously ever changing world of information technology (IT) and the new unforeseeable options each new generation of IT presents. These relationship management risks are not an integral part of agency theory but are very real. Figure 6.1 shows where these new risks come in along the IS outsourcing timeline. In this chapter we shall discuss the risks of managing this relationship. Here, too, one of the key aspects, as it is throughout the process of IS outsourcing, is to continuously invest in knowing and controlling risks. This is easier said than done, but it is essential. This chapter will discuss some aspects of how to do so.

Some Aspects of Managing the Relationship With the Agent

We discussed agency risks in chapter 4. To these risks it is now time to add risks in setting up the contractual relationship itself and risks about managing this contractual relationship after the appropriate agent has, or agents have, been selected in phase 3 in Figure 6.1. Setting up the nature of the relationship and how it will be managed is a crucial part of IS outsourcing because the relationship, both in its contractual aspects and in those aspects that go beyond the contract itself, is both one of the tools of controlling risks and one of the sources of additional risks. Through the contract the principal can add risk controls, for example, through the inclusion of quality monitoring standards such as CMMI or ISO 9000. But in specifying these contractual risk control details in the contract the principal may inadvertently also open the door to new risks, such as the agent following these contractual requirements to the letter only, and so adding the risk that the agent may not invest in keeping up to date with market trends and possibilities. Or the agent may choose

Adding to Agency

Figure 6.1. Timeline of risks.

not to invest in acquiring new capabilities and knowledge beyond what the contract demands. Likewise, delineating in the contract which key personnel the agent will assign to the project (a clause used quite often in time and materials contracting), and having exact specifications, service-level agreement (SLA), and schedule are all important. But once changes need to be made these contractual safeguards may be used against the principal, in that the agent may follow them as contractually required without caring about notifying the principal if things could be done better by changing these obligations. And so, while contractual controls can control known risks in the present, the very specifying of these controls can potentially produce new risks in the future. Managing these contract setup risks requires paying attention, among other things, to several points:

1. The contract should include within it the mechanism for managing and administering changes. This might include incentives, even informal ones, for the agent to suggest improvements.

2. Built into the relationship should be the knowledge that it is a win-win situation, so that it will always be in the interest of both parties to maintain it and not take short-term advantage of the situation or leave it altogether when a better opportunity arises. It should be a long-term relationship with strong incentives built into the contract to ensure this

long-term orientation. The example of the bank creating such a situation by letting its software agents know they have a higher chance of being contracted on a time and materials basis only after having many previous successful contracts,[3] is one way of doing so.

3. It is imperative to have a conflict resolution mechanism built into the contract. This should include how things are measured, the lack of which is one of the major causes of conflict, and a process by which resolution of conflict issues is first attempted by lower-level project managers and the issues are then escalated gradually to higher and higher-level managers in an orderly and agreed-upon fashion.

4. There should also be built-in reporting mechanisms so all parties and all involved personnel with authority know exactly where things stand at any given point in time on the schedule so there are no surprises. Having Gantt or Pert charts, or equivalent methodology, for doing so is a good idea. This includes, by the way, also documenting all the measures of all the CSFs on an agreed-upon schedule, as well as an agreed-upon method of documenting problems and conflicts and what was done about them at each step. Figure 4.3 is the result of such a mechanism of documenting all the software problem reports during the Y phase of an X+Y contract. This documentation saved the vendor I worked for quite an embarrassment when the chief executive officer (CEO) of the client claimed we had too many bugs in the software.

5. Most important, there should be clear boundaries of responsibilities between the principal and the agent.

In addition, the principal and the agent should be of about equal size so each will take the other seriously, unless the IS service being outsourced is standardized to such a degree that there is little room for power plays.

The issue here is that the contract, and within it also the SLA, must be done correctly or else the relationship cannot be managed based upon it. In addition, there must be clear expectation management, accurate specifications, detailed measureable service levels, delivery times, and no misunderstandings about costing and intellectual property (IP) rights. The contract must be done correctly or else the relationship cannot be managed based on it.

Keep It Small and Manageable

In at least partly addressing these risks Matta and Ashkenas[4] observed that IS projects overall are often too complex, and so might be better managed by splitting larger projects into small projects, or, as they call it, "rapid results initiatives." This is indeed a common practice in industry.[5] Applying this approach, IS managers can better identify problems, create buy-in, recognize where there may be missing specs, and, most important, shift responsibility from senior managers to cross-sectional teams that comprise not only IS experts. Such projects are results oriented; small and fast and pilot oriented, they probably serve as much to alleviate people issues with the new IS through the vertical cross-functional organizational units as they simplify and improve the IS project management and development process. Perhaps inadvertently, Matta and Ashkenas hit on one of the key teachings of Sun Tsu here:

> When you engage in actual fighting, if victory is long in coming, the men's weapons will grow dull and their ardor will be dampened. If you lay siege to a town, you will exhaust your strength, and if the campaign is protracted, the sources of the state will not be equal to the strain. Never forget: When your weapons are dulled, your ardor dampened, your strength exhausted, and your treasure spent, other chieftains will spring up to take advantage of your extremity. Then no man, however wise, will be able to avert the consequences that must ensue.[6]

The same overall concept, keeping IS small and simple and every stakeholder involved, has been shown empirically with IS within the organization.[7]

Understand the Dynamics of the Agent

Extending that logic, the agent is arguably a stakeholder as well and should be made part of the process, which itself should be broken into small and quickly attainable projects. But things are not quite that simple when managing the agent. This is more than just knowing yourself and your enemy as Sun Tsu, introduced in chapter 1, said. It is a matter of managing the relationship with the programming team of the agent, too. The words of Kipling quoted at the beginning of this chapter emphasize the right mind-set. The agent is not your enemy, but it is not your employee, either. It is a third party upon whom you depend to jointly achieve a mission. So it is unwise to emphasize the difference between "you fellows" and "I." It is better to manage the relationship as a joint activity, which in reality it is. In doing so, it is also advisable to treat the agent's management (the bishops), who manage the business side and whose interest is in making money, differently from the way their programmers (the poor parish priests), who actually do the work, are treated. The agent's management should be treated politely but with distance. They are managers and politicians. The principal should not be so naïve as to think that the agent's management is its friend. The agent's management is responsible for its own business interests, including making a profit out of the relationship. But in the case of IS this is not always so with the agent's technical staff, who often do care about the quality of their work to a greater extent than they are required to by the agent's management. While the agent's management members are likely to be savvy early majority managers who see things in terms of return on investment (ROI), the programmers are often artisans who are proud of their work and often behave as innovators going the extra mile just to make a better artifact. And, most important, as a principal you should lead the relationship by example: respect the agent and the work of their programmers ("don't ride over seed"), show dignity and control ("keep your temper"), and be trustworthy through and through ("never tell 'em a lie").

Transparency

Another important point often not mentioned, but that as a project manager on the agent's side I have noticed, is the need for the principal to be open and transparent about its problems and requirements. This is a risky proposition and is not always advisable or practical. But when it is possible there are advantages to the principal being transparent. When the bidding agents know the principal is being transparent they will take a smaller safety margin on their bid price and schedule; it also encourages competition among these agents that should result in cheaper prices and possibly higher quality. Besides, if the agents know better what the principal needs then less-qualified agents will be less inclined to bid and the bid prices will be more realistic. And then, as the adage goes, what goes around comes around. If the principal creates an atmosphere of secrecy then the agents will do the same, exacerbating the agency risks based on information asymmetry. Likewise, during the IS outsourced project itself, if the principal is transparent then the agent will know better what it needs to do and so be less defensive in relying on the contract alone to determine what it needs to do. This willingness to go beyond the requirements of the contract should be advantageous to the principal because sometimes the agent needs to go out on a limb for the principal to make sure things are done properly.

Theoretically, a company should align its IS strategy, outsourcing included, with the contract and share this knowledge with its agents. This is true of IS policy[8] and this is true of outsourcing.[9] Practically, this is harder than it sounds because strategy is often the result of compromises. Typically, the chosen outsourcing specs and strategy are at best the least bad option most of the stakeholders can agree on. But since this strategy is implemented through the IS, at least the workflow and control sections of it, it is through the IS that these problems become evident, and it is the IS that are blamed for it. Needless to say, when the IS are outsourced matters are exacerbated. That is why some academic research emphasizes the need to be open and share this knowledge with the agent.[10] It is a matter of at least not introducing new risks.

Taking Steps to Control Cost Contractual Risks

Outsourcing in many cases is about saving costs, but this is not always achievable. There are many reasons for this, some of which relate to the way the contract setup and ongoing management are done. In order for an IS outsourcing contract to cut costs the portfolio must be specified and each line item must be budgeted.[11] This is setting the bar rather high for IS projects. IS projects, as a matter of reality, should be managed with the assumption that there are always missing specs and topics and that nobody actually read and understood all the 5,000-plus pages in the specs document. Thus, it may be asking too much of an IS manager to be able to accurately estimate the line item cost of every aspect of the outsourced IS project.

The cost-cutting objective may be missed because of the reality of how IS project costing is actually done, which adds even more inaccuracy to these estimates. I saw this in many cases I took part in. The way outsourced IS projects are often run is that, when the requirements are made, additional features are added to make sure all the stakeholders of interest get what they want. This is done to gain their approval and inflates the specifications of the project. Only then does the project leader estimate the cost and secure a budget at this estimated cost level, probably with a little safety margin added. This budget is secured through the chief financial officer (CFO), accounts payable, or equivalent, depending on the budget required and organizational regulations. The budget is secured, although the CFO may approve less budget than the IS project manager requested. Once the tender is published, however, and the bids come in higher than the original estimated cost—because the CFO allocated less budget than requested or the IS project manager was overly optimistic in estimating the costs or more specs were added after the budget was approved—the project is often cut to size to remain within the original budgetary constraints and to avoid reopening the budget, which would require a new approval by the CFO or equivalent. If this process of cutting the project down to size so it can meet the budget is not managed properly then chances are the project will need to be expanded later on (possibly in the Y component of an X+Y contract) to include those modules that were taken out. However, adding these modules at this advanced stage in the project will likely cost more if only because already-written and tested modules need to be rewritten and tested. The result would be that the IS outsourced project will cost more than originally expected and therefore not achieve the expected cost savings.

Blaming the agent or expecting it to pick up the slack in such cases should be avoided. Taking advantage of keeping the IS outsourced project small and manageable could come in handy in this case, too, as well as be transparent with the agent who will find this out anyway sooner or later. One of the ways to manage the process of such escalations and de-escalations in the IS outsourced project scope is by introducing measureable expectation of the agent.

Adding Measureable CSFs to the Contract

The contract is the formal basis of the legal relationship between the principal and the agent. It is also the informal basis for the many other things that are happening in an outsourced IS project beyond what is explicitly stipulated in the contract and thus determines the nature of the relationship. This is why, apart from good management, the contract must specify the explicit CSF measures for each milestone, how they will be measured, what the critical values of each are, and, possibly, what actions need to be taken when the CSF measures do not meet their required values. Including the measures of the CSFs in the contract, apart from being good management, sends an important message to the agent about the nature of the relationship and the professionalism of the principal. The measurement of the CSFs should also include those parts of the project the principal allows the agent to subcontract to other agents. This too sends a clear message to the agent of exactly what the principal requires. Adding these CSF measures is not a matter of showing distrust toward the agent. On the contrary, it is so much easier for the agent to deliver successfully when the criteria are explicit. Moreover, explicit CSF measures allow the agent to protect itself from surprises and changing specs, and thus to bid at a lower price. This is because the agent probably expects this IS project to be no different from typical IS projects where the project is allotted a limited budget, often a very optimistic one; and so, when push comes to shove and the bid prices come in above the expected budget things need to be taken out of the specifications so the project can nonetheless be let out. But, by taking out sections to allow the project to remain within budgetary limits, the risk of missing and inconclusive specifications increases. If the CSF measures of the delivery criteria are made explicit, however, the agent can make the point that these missing specs are indeed missing specs rather than programming errors. This allows the agent to control its own risks. This is crucial because the mind-set of the agent's management is also attuned to controlling risks.

Adding measureable CSFs also makes the job of the agent's project leaders easier because it allows the agent to shift the responsibility of unclear strategy and dealing with conflicting stakeholder demands and lack of understanding among the users to the principal. Dealing with such risks requires a person who can extinguish fires without making a mess. These leaders are unique and the agent probably has only a limited number of such proficient managers.

Moreover, it is estimated that setting up and running such demand management among the users may cost 2% to 10% of the contract price,[12] which may be more than the client realizes. Being explicit in the contract about the appropriate measureable CSFs and quality service levels is one way of controlling these risks.

All this is important for the principal as well, because the more risks the agent has the less likely it is that the really good agents—who have many other tenders to choose from—will bid on this tender. And those agents who do bid on it may bid higher than they would have otherwise in order to cover these additional risks.

An important caveat here is that although the CSF measures must be monitored continually, and when possible not only during milestone delivery, the principal must be careful not to overdo it. It is important not to micromanage the IS outsourcing relationship, because that will destroy the necessary trust between principal and agent. It is also important to give the agent some leeway to correct its mistakes without washing its dirty linen in public. As important as monitoring is for risk control, sometimes within a very limited degree it is better to turn a blind eye, because if the agent loses face it will be less effective toward the principal's users and its own employees. Mistakes will happen. Do not expect the impossible. What can be done, nonetheless, is to have a principal liaison project officer in charge sitting at the agent's site providing ongoing review of the process. This principal liaison should not be the same person the principal assigns to be the service delivery manager as this may cause too much conflict of interests.

Addressing Agent Employee Turnover in the Contract

An unavoidable risk in long-term IS projects is employee turnover. The principal must always ask what happens if key agent personnel are moved by the agent to another of its clients or if they leave the agent to seek employment elsewhere. In both cases this could result in a lack of continuity among the employees the agent assigns to the project—with all the negative consequences this may have on work quality, meeting deadlines, loss of tacit knowledge, and relationship management with users, as well as the bad impression it may create among the principal's stakeholders not only of the agent but of their own IS project manager. To some extent the contract can be used to control these risks by (a) stipulating in the contract who the key agent personnel assigned to it should be and how many hours a week on average they are expected to devote to it, and (b) limiting the duration of the contract. Indeed, Gartner recommends not signing long-term IS outsourcing projects; and it is reported that Linda Cohen, vice president and distinguished analyst at Gartner, said: "Don't sign long-term deals, there won't be enduring value for you or for your service provider. The days of the ten year deals are long gone."[13] This problem might be especially acute when offshoring, where it is reported that employee turnover at software vendors may be as high as 30%.[14]

Addressing IP Issues, Confidentiality, and Noncompete Clauses

Another aspect of managing the relationship with the agent is realizing that it is a time-limited contract. An integral part of managing the agent should therefore be what happens after the contract comes to its conclusion. Specifically, the contract should specify who owns the IP so it is clear who owns the IS and the knowledge developed during the outsourcing process, to ensure confidentially so information held by the agent is controlled, and to demand noncompete clauses so the agent cannot use the knowledge it gained from this contract to compete with the principal or provide equivalent services to the principal's competition.

Because of this it is common practice that IS outsourcing contracts specify who owns the IP and require all agent employees involved to sign confidentiality, nondisclosure, and noncompete clauses as part of the contract. This of course does not mean the agent's employees will unlearn what they learned in the project, and it does not mean they will not reuse what they have learned in providing services to other principals. All it means, practically speaking, is that the same software and algorithms will not be used. This opens up a new set of risks to the principal. The story of SABRE, the American Airlines reservation booking system, is an example of reapplying knowledge learned elsewhere without breaking the law. Apparently, at least according to some reports of the story, IBM had just completed a somewhat similar system for the U.S. Air Force on their semi-automatic ground environment (SAGE) project[15] and reused their learned experience on SABRE.[16]

The principal should be aware of these risks and consider taking steps to limit them, for example, by splitting the outsourced project into many smaller projects so no one agent can see the forest for the trees. Outsourcing does not solve the issue of data confidentiality, either, as some embarrassing cases that have come to press show.[17] Again, steps to protect the principal and its clientele must be considered in the contract.

Writing the Contract to Lock-in the Agent

It is impossible to fully control for all these risks through the contract alone. Industry reports highlight such problems associated with unrealistic expectations. These include overly optimistic timetables to transfer knowledge and poor communication between the principal and the agent. They also include situations where objectives are not explicit or are primarily only about cutting costs, where the agent's sales team overpromises or the principal creates imprecise contracts, and there is rapid turnover among agent employees.[18] That is why some principals devise ways of ensuring vendor lock-in, that is, making it worthwhile for the agent to go out of its way to make the principal happy, to stick it out instead of just leaving to seek greener pastures. One such method is described in Gefen and colleagues,[19] where the principal, a large European bank, allotted the less risky time and materials contracts primarily to agents who had accumulated lots of previously successful projects.

I was told of the same kind of arrangement from the vendor side, too. The director of sales of a software services vendor in Philadelphia told me that although almost all their contracts nowadays are fixed price, when they do get a time and materials contract it is only because the client had been working with them and the particular person they had asked for and had known them for years. Familiarity built trust. Having identified them and this person as someone they could trust, the client decided to contract on a time and materials basis to reduce its transaction costs overhead and control its risk. The relationship became a win-win situation thanks to its long-term perspective and because it was based on trust. Other methods include allowing only a select cadre of agents to bid on the IS outsourcing contracts of the principal so that these few agents who are in this select group have an incentive to remain in it.[20]

Know What You Want

To some extent it really comes down to the basic question of whether the principal is outsourcing to cut its IS ownership costs as a *late majority* manager might, à la Carr,[21] or whether it is doing so to acquire new capabilities à la the *technology imperative* suggested in this book. In the former case it is about standardization and cost savings. It is about financial risk control. It is not about having a contract that might lead to better management of the relationship with the agent. The contract deals with standard IS and therefore technical risk, and the need to rely on the agent going the extra mile for the principal is not a key issue. After all, if the agent does not deliver on these predefined and readily available IS services, there are plenty of other agents that will. This is where outsourcing e-mail service management to a vendor, such as Gmail, or outsourcing the management of terabytes of memory comes in. In these cases the contract is quite the same as any other interfirm contract, and the outsourcing of IS is not really that special.

In the latter case when outsourcing is done to acquire new capabilities, on the other hand, outsourcing is about achieving shorter time to market, increasing flexibility, gaining knowledge the IT department does not currently have, and increasing ability by gaining experienced personnel the company does not have. This is where IS outsourcing is different. The contract in this case is about delegating responsibility to the agent and the principal retaining only an arm's-length control through measureable CSFs. The principal depends on the agent to follow not only the letter but also the spirit of the contract. The contract should also focus on creating the correct atmosphere with the agent, which is what this chapter is about.

One should not mix the two types of context. In both cases treating IS outsourcing as a panacea or only thinking of the principal's side is wrong, but more so in the latter case. Likewise, the contract serves more than just a legal purpose in both cases, but more so in the latter. Legal recourse in both cases should be treated as a last resort. After all, put yourself in the seat of the IS project manager of the principal and ask yourself whose head will roll if the contract fails? Surely, at least part of the blame will lie with the IS project manager who chose this agent and signed the contract with this agent in the first place, but, again, more fault will lie with the principal's IS project manager in the latter case. And in both cases an attitude of "do it for me" without oversight is a mistake, although more so in the latter.

People Being Cognitively Challenged Risks

All these risks, and many others, are compounded by the fact that it might be too much to expect that the people involved on both the principal and the agent sides will not be *cognitively challenged*. Being cognitively challenged means not being clever enough to see the whole picture of the IS and how everything is supposed to be interrelated within the system and the other systems it relates to until the IS are up are running—and sometimes not even then. In transaction cost economics this is also known as *bounded rationality*. People are not clever enough and have limited understanding and memory to really comprehend what is happening.[22]

Bounded rationality may explain why IS contracts are incomplete at the onset and why therefore there are risks of unforeseen contingencies.[23] The reality of IS and the organizations that use them is simply too complex to easily map out in sufficient detail. There are too many stakeholders with competing requirements and CSFs, and these stakeholders may be uncertain themselves of their own requirements. In addition, there are always unforeseen contingencies, which may stem from new technologies, users realizing the mistakes they made, new possibilities once the IS are implemented, or the need in some industries to address new government requirements. Ex post facto renegotiations, suggested by some textbook solutions,[24] are seldom done in the industry. In reality, the industry prefers short outsourcing contracts, preferably fixed price, and addressing new requirements with new contracts. Renegotiation is rarely done. Changes to specs when signing a new contract are not practical. They are often managed through maintenance contracts, which in enterprise resource planning (ERP), for example, may cost annually 10% to 15% of original implementation costs of the ERP system.

Figure 4.2 demonstrates the consequences of bounded rationality. The data presented there come from one of the projects I managed. In that project we ran the new IS we had implemented in parallel with the old IS so the client and we, the vendor, could verify that everything worked okay. To our surprise, a large percentage of the mismatched errors between the two IS ended up being due to bugs in the original IS, which had been running at that stage for at least 10 years. With only delayed manual checking of errors in the old IS, apparently, no one discovered those bugs. These errors and those relating to missed issues in the original specifications document accounted for almost half the software problem reports we dealt with in the first 6 months after releasing the new IS. And, emphasizing the cognitive challenge, this was an experienced client who had an adequately large and very good team of industrial engineers and managers who checked every detail of the project and to whom this was by no means the first large IS development and implementation they were overseeing. It is unrealistic to expect managers, programmers, or even systems analysts to comprehend all the intricacies of even a short, 5,000-page requirements document.

Steps in Managing the Contractual Relationship With the Agent

Step 1: Do Your Homework Before You Begin

So, how should the agent be managed through the contract? The first step begins long before the agent has been chosen. As an IS project manager working for the principal you must first analyze in detail exactly what is needed and achieve consensus among the stakeholders about these objectives and their measureable CSFs. Once the requirements document is ready, estimate the cost of developing the IS project in-house. Do so even if you have every intention of outsourcing it because you are doing this to understand the costing of each aspect of it. It would be advisable at this stage to have several experienced systems analysts and project managers independently provide estimates so you can gauge the reliability of this estimate. It might be a good idea to have both systems analysts and project managers give estimates because each profession sees IS projects differently: the former in terms of how the system is going to be used and with this the problems in its implementation and the latter in terms of developing and installing the IS.

If the estimates more or less converge and you are satisfied that the systems analysts and project managers understand it the same way, then add a safety margin by revising their average estimate upward to make it realistic. Twenty-five percent would not be too much as there are always things that have been left out. If possible, it may be advisable at this stage to give out the requirements document to a few trusted agents you have worked with in the past and ask them for a nonbinding estimate of the requirements document as a draft. This may be an iterative process where you continually drop features from the requirements and reestimate costs to bring the project to within approximately how much the CFO or accounts payable will allow you to spend on this contract. This may also require renegotiating with the various stakeholders to gain their approval for this reduced scope.

At this stage you go to accounts payable or to the CFO and request budgetary approval for the project on this estimated cost. There will probably be a legally approved bid selection procedure you must follow, but it will almost certainly contain an RFP and maybe also an RFI beforehand. An RFI is a request for information. An RFP is a request for proposal or an actual bid on this tender. An RFP is also known as a tender and as a RFQ, or request for quote.

Step 2: Publish an RFI and RFP

The objective of an RFI is to identify potential suppliers, that is, agents, while making no commitment on behalf of the principal to actually issue a tender, although it is understood that such a tender is probable. The RFI lets the principal know more about the market and who the agents in it are. An RFP, on the other hand, implies commitment by the principal that there will be a bidding process on an explicit scope of work (SOW) and schedule. The RFP has a detailed SLA and terms and conditions. The RFP should also contain within it the selection and evaluation criteria and timelines, as well as confidentiality issues. In addition, some companies allow agents to call or to attend a vendor conference to ask questions about the SOW, SLA, and RFP.

Examples of RFI can be found online at federal government sites. The RFI often begins by stating the commitment of the principal to the project, its vision and objectives, and the reasons for the project, as well as an estimated SOW. The RFI may also include nondetailed requirements as well as some details about the anticipated deliverables and the acceptance criteria on these deliverables. These details are included so that the agents will have an idea if they are suitable for the task. In addition, the RFI may contain a more detailed requirements document and the types of expertise and certifications the agents should have. The objective of an RFI is twofold: to allow the principal to learn what agents operate in the market and to let the agents know that an RFP may be coming out soon so they can prepare.

The RFP must specify exactly what is needed and the quality measures required. The RFP should start with a cover letter specifying what this is all about and why the principal requests the proposal. The remainder of the RFP will typically include the following:

1. A description of the principal's organization: a description of the company, what it does, where it does it, how much is done at each location and how many employees are involved, what it currently has, and any other information relevant to the SOW.

2. A detailed list of the project's objectives.

3. Project governance, such as whether it will be fixed price or time and materials, whether there are penalties and rewards, and whether or not the agent is requested to provide cost of any additional services.

4. Details of the requested work in an SOW and its master service agreement (MSA) combined with a more detailed description of the required service quality in an SLA. If applicable, this section may also include requirements at each location.

5. Measurable CSFs and their critical values of the SOW, MSA, and SLA. This section may also have detailed requirements and specifications including both delivery and payment milestones and the exact deliverables due at each milestone together with their quality assurance measures and acceptance criteria, possibly including expected savings.

6. Details of the bidding process, such as how to submit the bid, what to include in it, what not to include, and possible issues of confidentiality such as not divulging information about this RFP. This section may also include a timeline of the bid selection process.

7. Contact information for inquiries at the principal.

8. What information you require of the bidding agent, including price, track record, key personnel to be involved, details of related products

and services the agent delivers, suggested warranties, maintenance agreements if applicable, and the contact person at the agent.

9. How to deal with unforeseen contingencies, additional requirements, changes in the specifications, and emergency treatments.

10. There should also be a conflict resolution addendum that specifies how disputes are recorded—for example, through a system that records software problem reports—and a mechanism to periodically report these problems, as well as a mechanism to immediately report cases that require immediate attention. Most such problems may be managed by those directly involved, but in some cases it may be necessary to bring in top management, too. In this case there should be a predefined mechanism, specified already in the RFP, of a management hierarchy of disputes resolution beginning with periodic weekly meetings between the project leaders of the principal and the agent, and a backup mechanism bringing it up to senior management, the board of directors, if relevant, and, finally, details of legal resolution or arbitration about the project.

Government and large companies have explicit process and formulations of RFP. There must be no nepotism in the process. At least in a government RFP, the process must be open at this stage. The RFP process may also include a mechanism for agents to contact the project manager at the principal to ask questions and may have a mechanism to share these answers with all competing agents. The RFP will contain explicit eligibility criteria. Examples of RFP can be found online at federal government sites.[25]

Again, throughout this RFI and RFP process the objectives are reducing and controlling the risks the principal faces. One must clarify as much as possible what the agent is facing so it too can calculate and reduce its own risks. The agent can thereby apply only to appropriate RFP, reducing the adverse selection risks of the principal, and apply with a smaller safety margin, reducing the overall cost to the principal.

Before the principal publishes the RFI and RFP it should decide if this will be an open bid with many vendors, as government RFPs are sometimes required to be, or a tender with only one or a select number of trusted vendors, as chief information officers (CIOs) of private companies interviewed for this book prefer. At any rate, the decision will not be all about price, and it must be a win-win situation. This is a complex process. If this is the first time the principal has done this, it might be advisable to consider hiring a sourcing advisor. It may also be at this stage that the principal decides it might be better to do the project in-house after all, because it realizes that the transaction costs in soliciting and selecting agents may be too high. Next, the principal uses its own lawyers or it hires lawyers to write the contract. The contract must be in legal terms and will probably contain things a project manager might not usually be aware of such as IP and damages.

Also advisable is to document and keep track of everything done in the process. This might be a good idea not only because regulations require it but also because this is a good way to accumulate a good practices database. Indeed, there is a tendency among new buyers to open the tender to many bids, and after locating one they really trust to open the bid initially only to this one vendor. This is known as *private bidding*.[26] Private bidding, when allowed, can cut transaction costs in reviewing and selecting bids, reduce the cost of risk in trying a new vendor, and avoid the learning costs a new agent may incur. All said, although the bid price may be higher in a private bid—and we know from other markets that agents do take advantage of private bids to bid higher [27]—it may still be cheaper to have a private bid considering its reduced transaction costs. There is a trade-off here. A sole agent may lower transaction costs and allow faster selecting, but it may not be the cheapest or best solution and the agent may take advantage of the situation. Moreover, having competitive bidding should drive market prices down and should force the agents to pay more attention to the quality of the solution they are proposing, and to assign more qualified personnel to it. Having competitive bidding also helps the principal learn more about the market and the various options available. The one solution the principal is locked on to may not be the only, or the best, one. However, competitive bidding does take longer and has higher transaction costs, and the competing agents will charge a higher price themselves to account for their own transaction costs and risk of not winning the tender.

Step 3: Eliminate Outliers

Once the RFP has been published and bids come in, then it is time to choose among the bids. But before this is done another risk control should be applied. At this stage the principal project manager should review the prices in the bids. First, remove all the bids that are extremely low priced, which may indicate the agent did not understand the RPF or is too desperate. Then, remove all the bids that are too high priced, which may suggest the agent is taking advantage of the situation. As a footnote, removing those agents who might be lowballing (i.e., charging way below market price) is also advisable. Such agents may raise their prices once they achieve principal lock-in,[28] taking advantage of the high switching costs of the principal and its interest to avoid the transaction costs of identifying another reasonable agent.[29] Next, the principal's project manager should examine the mode price and the average price of the remaining bids. If the mode and average prices are approximately in the range of the original price estimate given to the CFO, then the project managers can pat themselves on the back. This may indicate that they and the bidding agents have approximately the same understanding of the requirements.

Chances are, however, that the estimate of the principal did not match the mode price. In this case it might be advisable to contact some of the agents and ask them what their costing function was. In other words, how did they arrive at the price they bid? It would be unadvisable to just say the market mode is so and so and therefore I will accept it. If the market mode is not what you expected, then chances are either you do not fully understand the cost of the requirements or you wrongly specified them. The principal also wants to make sure that the agent also makes a reasonable profit. At any rate, it would look bad to go back to the CFO and say I need another 20% on the estimated cost. It would look worse still to say I can deliver at 20% less than expected, because this would broadcast that you do not understand pricing and the next time you ask for a budget you will only be given 80% of what you asked for. Moreover, if the agent can deliver at 20% less than your estimate, and you did your estimate properly, then the agent might be underbidding to win and lose money on the project, which is known as the *winner's curse*. This might mean that the agent will end up cutting corners so it does not lose too much on the project, and any cutting corners in software development or implementation could mean an increased chance of bugs.

At any rate, choosing the winning bid should not be a matter of price alone. Price is always important because the bottom line is always, literally, the bottom line. But it is not only about price when it concerns software or IS. Apart from bid price, the project manager at the principal should check the track record of each contending agent. This is important not only as a matter of checking on their capabilities but also because one of the crucial concerns of principals is whether the agent will still be around in a few years' time.[30] Apart from obtaining the agent's track record as a company, it may also be necessary to interview the key personnel the agent is proposing to put on the project. Interviewing can be quite an expensive endeavor if many bids make it to the short list, so it is advisable to eliminate as many agents as possible before that happens. *Interviews are important because ultimately it is these senior programmers, database administrators (DBAs), and project managers on whom the success of the outsourcing project depends.* And it is precisely because one senior programmer or DBA or project manager is not the same as any other that it may well be that a nominally more expensive bid in monetary terms might actually be practically cheaper considering the personnel the agent promises to put on the project. It is customary that software engineers and programmers be paid different tariffs based on their education, software and hardware specialties, certifications, and years of experience. But it is not only formal qualifications and experience that counts. A more expensive bid may actually be cheaper because it is primarily their capabilities and experience as software artisans that the principal counts on. No certification really captures this genius, and only their track record and maybe interviews can reveal this. That is why it is imperative to interview, and not just rely on certifications and other superficial exams. A principal can also learn a lot about the agent company itself by interviewing these key personnel.

Next, the principal should check to see if the bid itself is professionally done. If the bid skims over important issues, is not written properly, does not address all the information required in the RFP, and so on, then there might be reason for concern. Basically, if the agent does not do a good job of preparing the bid and is not pedantic about its details, then this may be indicative of the agent's culture and how it gets things done—and a principal should certainly not want any lack of attention to detail in the programmers it hires. Besides, a lack of respect to the process at this early stage could indicate lack of respect in the next stages, too, and the principal has enough risks to take care of already in the outsourcing process without adding this as another primary risk. The high cost of IS failure, increased by inattentive agents, should not be ignored.

There is also the question of whether the agent provides a reasonable justification for its costing, that is, based on what price it assigns to each important aspect of the bid. In the case of software development this mostly includes personnel time. If the agent is open about its costing and staffing, this may indicate the agent's honesty. This is crucial because the last thing a principal wants is an agent who cannot be trusted. Indeed, in examining the cost-benefit evaluation clients made of their relationship with a software vendor, an ERP customization in one study, we found that this evaluation depended mostly on the perception that the vendor was trustworthy in its dealings with them.[31] Trust was as important in this evaluation as the perceived usefulness of the ERP after customization,[32] which is what the vendor was contracted to do in the first place.

Step 4: Make a Choice

At this stage, the IS project manager at the principal has eliminated bids that are too high or too low and those that just do not look professional. Now, its CSFs should be (a) quality, (b) being on time, and (c) user satisfaction. Unless regulations force otherwise, the principal should ignore minor price differences. What the principal should concentrate on is evaluating the track record and key personnel of the bidding agents and if they are financially sound. Requesting recommendations if the agent is a small vendor would be advisable, as well as having a pre-set list of CSFs for the choice of this agent, although one should allow for the list's modification as the principal's team learns how to make the choice better. A pre-set list makes managing the process easier because it avoids the impression of one team member at the principal maybe showing favoritism or relying on irrelevant impressions. It also allows the accumulation of a best practices database so the principal can learn from its experience.

Another consideration worth thinking about at this stage is how to eventually end the relationship with the agent. Having an equivalent of a "prenuptial agreement" and choosing an agent who agrees to this is a good idea. If the agent does not agree to this, then the principal should be suspicious. Any IS outsourcing contract is limited by time, and without such an agreement there may be reason to suspect that the agent is trying to create client lock-in or is just not professional. In either case, it may be advisable for the principal to reduce its risks by avoiding such agents. There are enough risks as it is. This agreement basically says how the contracting relationship will end and who owns what and owes what.

Related to the issue of a "prenuptial agreement" is the need to have a specifications-changing mechanism agreed upon already at this stage in the agent selection process. This is especially important in the case of IS outsourcing because these contracts and the requirements they support can be expected to change over time, as Figure 4.3 shows. It is imperative, therefore, to include a change or an adjustment mechanism in the contract so that when changes need to be made to the contract there is an agreed-upon mechanism for doing so[33]—and, most important, choose an agent who is aware of the need to do so and knows how to.

If possible, it is advisable especially at this stage when it is no longer about the technical ability of the agent—which is typically agreed by all to be a proprietary issue of the IS project manager—to include all the major stakeholders in the decision-making process. This is important for a variety of reasons. First of all, it is a matter of politics. IS projects, outsourced ones included, fail primarily because of people problems rather than technology ones. Technology problems may delay delivery and add to costs, but they are mostly solvable. People's resistance and distrust, on the other hand, cannot be solved by just throwing more money at the project. Having the stakeholders involved reduces their resistance. It also allows for the inclusion of more viewpoints in the decision-making process and with it a better understanding of the processes the client organization has. This inclusion also builds trust and a sense of justice and reduces animosity and distrust, which is crucial because the project is going to run into difficulties and these will be exacerbated if the stakeholders distrust the project leader or have doubts about the process. Basically, when things go wrong, and every now and then they will, others will be less critical of the project and its leader if they participate in the process, as we also showed empirically.[34]

During this process there are bound to be disputes and misunderstandings about the ability of the various agents and the bids they posted. Rather than guess what an agent meant or take the approach that if the agent made a mistake then they can pay for it, it might be advisable to be open with the agent about your process and expectations, and ask them for details about these points. This not only reduces tension within the team choosing the agents and shows due diligence, important in its own right, it also allows for the creation of a better working relationship with the agent in the future. Indeed, according to some industry sources one of the most frequent reasons outsourcing fails is that the principal does not have clear expectations upfront (23% of the cases) or that the interests of the principal and the agent become unaligned over time (15% of the cases).[35] This is also part of the broader issue of transparency discussed earlier. The agents need to understand the principal and its expectation so the agent can give the principal better service and still make a profit. Besides, what goes around comes around. If the agent is treated like a partner, there is a better chance it will reciprocate accordingly and go the extra mile when necessary. And if the agent underbids because it did not understand the tender or because the principal misled the agent, then the agent will make up for it some other way and the principal will pay the price in reduced quality.

Understanding the agent is imperative in creating a win-win situation. This relates among other things to its delivery competency, as well as its ability to respond to the principal's operational needs, its performance, its cost, its quality, its robustness, and its flexibility. This also relates to the question of whether the quality of service will at least remain the same over time. Naturally, answering these questions also requires the principal to understand its own needs and objectives: what level of service is needed and whether the objective of the outsourcing agreement is to replace an existing IT with a better one or perhaps to free personnel to do other things. Most important, is the objective to find an agent who can be replaced easily or is this outsourcing agreement about a long-term relationship?[36]

Crucial also at this stage—as everywhere throughout the process—is to document the decision-making process. Every large project should have a postproject evaluation to identify lessons learned and mistakes made and how they could be avoided, to develop a best practices database, to learn how to improve the process for the next round, and to improve the evaluation criteria of the project. All this requires detailed documentation. Decisions should be documented when they are made, rather than later as subjective and biased post hoc recollections. Moreover, when people know their actions are documented they behave accordingly, so documenting is another way to ensure that the process is done correctly. And, most important, documentation allows the principal organization to evaluate its managers' performance and promote for success. This also plays well into Peter Drucker's observation: "If you can't measure it, you can't manage it."

The Contract Itself

The contract itself sets in place the details of the business relationship as well as the controls set to manage it. It also specifies the manner of communications to take place during the contractual period and the penalties and rewards, as well as expectations of both sides. The contract is a promise enforced by law of what is being promised, how much is being paid, and when and where the transaction will take place. Key elements in it are the specification of the products or services involved, including possible benchmarks, metrics, quality measures, and penalties. The contract will also include the pricing structure, such as fixed price or time and materials, the payment schedule and delivery milestones, and the contract duration.[37] Also included are the explicit and specific rights and responsibilities of all parties. In addition, the contract may contain the command structure and authority of the project, such as who issues orders and demands performance, and who does what, who reports to whom, and who can sign on what. The contract may also contain standard operating procedures (SOPs), a formal progress reporting mechanism, and explicit bylaws.[38] Perhaps no less important, contracts typically include an informal dispute resolution mechanism and institutional structures to manage the relationship.[39]

In addition, the contract sets the *psychology of the relationship*. This point about psychology deserves more attention than people who are not intimately acquainted with software development may realize, especially in the case of software development outsourcing. In software development outsourcing the requirements should be partly incomplete upfront, and changes in the specifications should therefore be expected as the IS is implemented. This amounts to an incomplete set of requirements, resulting in a need to rely on the agent to follow the spirit rather than the letter of the contract. Choosing an agent who can support such a relationship and not be overly pedantic about the details is essential in many cases of software development outsourcing. Nonetheless, even with such an agent the contract, and with it the SLA, should be as accurate and detailed as possible, and should leave a mechanism to deal with such changes so that the agent, following the spirit rather than the letter of the contract, does not need to absorb losses. As mentioned before, the agent probably wants the project to succeed and will go the extra mile beyond its contractual obligations to make sure it does, but if the agent is about to lose money in the process its attitude will change and it will cut corners—with the inevitable consequences to quality and increased bugs that the principal will eventually bear and pay the price for. One way of addressing this is by signing an X+Y contract, whereby these changes in the specs can be dealt with in the subsequent Y part of the contract where the agent is paid on the basis of time and materials. This too signals to the agent that the principal intends to be fair in its dealings.

It is also important to include in the contract, and in the RFP beforehand, whether the project will be implemented in a phased, pilot, parallel, or cold-turkey fashion. In a phased project the IS project is broken into modules and each module is implemented separately with significant periods of time between each module. This gives the project management team time to learn and improve, and therefore control their risks better, from one module implementation to the next. In a pilot project the project is released to one site at a time. This too gives the project management time to learn and improve, and therefore control their risks, as they implement the new IS in one site after another. Needless to say, project implementation can be managed as both phased and pilot, in which case the IS would be implemented at one site at a time and in each site one module at a time. In a parallel project implementation the new IS are released and run for some time while the old IS are still running. In effect there are two IS, the original one and the newly implemented one, each running on the same input at the same time. This option can control risk by providing an exit plan should something go wrong. In addition, by comparing the output of the two IS, it provides a measure of how correct the output and results of the new IS are. Here, too, the project implementation strategy can be (a) parallel and pilot, (b) parallel and phased, or (c) parallel and both pilot and phased. The alternative to these three options is implementing the new IS as a cold-turkey project, that is, replacing the old IS with the new one all at once. This option is not recommended because it introduces many avoidable risks. Whatever option is chosen, however, it should be made explicit in the contract. The more the principal lets it be known how it controls risk, the fewer safety margins the agents will take in their bidding price and the better prepared they will be for the outsourcing project.

Contractual controls are also critical. These controls fall into two categories. The *formal controls*, which is how controls are typically done, deal with explicit (written) ways to manage the relationship, including but not limited to the explicit obligations and responsibilities of both sides, timetables and with them delivery and payment milestones, penalties should these timetables be missed by either side, and quality controls such as testing and documentation. These controls are critical because by setting the rules they make it easier to manage the relationship, which is necessary considering that, according to some sources, 75% of managers in principal companies claim outsourcing did not meet their expectations and 76% said they lacked outsourcing managerial skills training.[40] These controls, however, are not really enough in the case of IS development outsourcing because of the incompleteness of the specs discussed earlier. This is why in these projects there is sometimes a need to rely on *informal controls*, such as shared values, peer pressure, social context, shared beliefs, rituals, and so on. These informal controls are harder to implement with outsourcing agents than when controlling internal IS development by the principal, and harder yet when the agent is abroad.

The level of the formal controls in the contract increases as the uncertainty of the outsourcing task increases, which may happen when it is harder to forecast the success of the project and the environment, and when the IS developed is more complex, unstructured, and nonroutine. On the other hand, the level of the formal controls will decrease as the principal becomes more knowledgeable about the IS and its context in both how closely the new IS are related to the core competency of the principal and when the principal has more technical knowledge and therefore knows better what to expect and how to present its requirements and feedback to the agent. Most important, formal controls decrease considerably more when the principal trusts the agent.[41] Trust is critical and has a stronger impact than any of the other factors discussed in this paragraph on the level of formal controls. It resonates well with the CIOs I interviewed for this book who kept on telling me of their preference to work with only a small cadre of agents with whom they had established a long-term trust-based relationship. It also resonates well with the decision of the bank discussed earlier,[42] that is, to encourage its software agents in a long-term relationship by presenting them with the prospect of the less risky time and materials contracts.

Contracts typically have a legal clause about the area of jurisdiction should the contract be breached. Nonetheless, resorting to the law is not a good option. First, there is only limited liability. Typically, the contract can only enforce damages for actual breach of contract and not for possible missed business opportunities had the software been delivered on time or within specs. Moreover, a small software vendor working as an agent for a large principal, such as a bank, cannot be expected to pay for large damage even if the principal could force that into the contract because the agent would just declare bankruptcy. At any rate, it would be questionable whether the principal, such as a bank, could avoid paying government fines for not implementing new requirements on time because the agent did not deliver the software on time. Thus, for example, by blaming a software vendor it employed, a bank could not avoid paying a fine to the Federal Reserve for not implementing new regulations. Second, legal action draws attention to the problems, hurting reputation and stock value even further. Third, it might create a name for the principal as a company that rushes to sue its agents. This would frighten away some potential agents and make others consider bidding at a higher price to account for their increased risk of being sued. Fourth, even if the principal wins in court, it takes time to run through the legal process, and it may cost so much in legal fees and executive time as to make the whole endeavor not worthwhile. And, most important, the principal as a company may have reason to sue the agent, but the IS project manager at the principal might have good reason not to do so: Chances are that if anything went wrong with the IS outsourcing project then at least part of the blame is on his or her head, and it is this head too that will roll because the outsourced project failed.

Some Points on How to Manage the Vendor

It is a truism that good fences make good neighbors. The same applies here, too. In managing the relationship with the agent it is imperative in the contract that the principal and the agent mark their respective domains clearly, that is, have unambiguously defined responsibilities for both sides. This starts in the contract and continues with the ongoing relationship. Although there is nothing new in saying so, it is amazing how many times these boundaries are crossed.

The first step to take, according to CIO roundtables we conducted, is to have a clearly defined SLA. This means that the SLA part of the contract must specify exactly what the principal wants and how it will be measured.[43] This also means having a clear map of the requirements before the tender is published, and if the principal does not know exactly what is needed then the principal should not outsource it. The contract should also articulate all the procedures, including conflict resolution and, when applicable, transfer protocol. Defining these mechanisms in the contract could avoid unnecessary friction. Progress report scheduling and the content of these reports should also be included in the contract. This reporting relates to both technical-level reporting to the project managers and strategic-level reporting to senior management at both the principal and the agent. The reporting should be of two kinds: scheduled progress reports and reports of unexpected problems and exceptions. Mechanisms of dealing with problems based on these reports should also be included, beginning with attempts to resolve these problems at the project management level, through how the issue may be escalated up to senior management, and then to binding arbitration.

The contract should also include explicit penalties and rewards to the agent as these relate to explicit performance measures of the agent. But these are really only methods of last resort. If the principal needs to apply a penalty to the agent, then the principal has not been managing the relationship correctly.

An integral part of the contract is the SLA. The SLA specifies the details of the required service levels. Because it allows the principal to communicate its expectations in detail it also serves indirectly to make sure the vendor is not going to lose money, Still, it is highly advisable to have a 30-day stop clause: If a new vendor does not deliver appropriately within the first 30 days, and this includes agreed-upon performance measures in the SLA, then the contract says drop him. Be aware, however, that things are never as simple as they seem. In practical terms this could also mean specifying in advance how the principal plans to monitor the agent, such as whether or not the principal plans to have on-site visits and their frequency. Having clear boundaries also includes whether and how the agent and the principal teams will be mixed or even shuttled from place to place.

Nonetheless, although the boundaries of responsibility need to be stressed with the agent on the managerial level, the principal should strive to make the agent's technical personnel part of the principal's own team— these are analogous to Kipling's poor parish priests in the epigraph to this chapter. These technical personnel should not be made to feel like outsiders, and treating them as part of the team is an essential way of not doing so. Treating them this way also helps warn the principal's IT managers early of any problems they may identify with the specs or the rest of the IS as they develop it and thus reduce surprises. This also helps keep the principal's own programmers and technical staff in the loop, which should alleviate their worries, too—a need quite a few CIOs did mention. *If there is one reason outsourced IS projects fail before they are deployed it is because of rampant distrust between the agent and the principal.* Once the agent no longer cares about the project and is just fulfilling its commitments by the book, it is a sure sign of problems on the horizon. Within reason, the principal must make sure things run in an atmosphere of trust. Setting the boundaries is one of the essential steps toward achieving this; striving to have the agent feel like part of the team is another way. Ruining trust leads to distrust, and that makes managing organizations harder because distrust results in employee skepticism and cynicism and an atmosphere of secrecy, blame, isolation, avoidance, passivity, and helplessness, as well as an attitude of doing just enough to get by with lack of involvement and, worse still, passing the blame around.[44] If not managed correctly, for example, if senior management resorts to enforcing tighter controls to get things moving, the result could be a vicious circle of even more distrust and with it even more negative behavior.[45] This is true even more so in outsourced IS projects. Therefore, having a policy of transparency and always being truthful is imperative in such projects, even if lawyers may advise otherwise. Managing the relationship and trust is crucial.[46]

And have short-term contracts. That controls risk and lets you learn from experience. It also breaks early any cycle of distrust.

Again, although money is always an important aspect of IS outsourcing, it is not the whole story. In fact, project managers interviewed for this book point out that agents are willing to lose money on their first contracts so long as they can build relationships and a long-term partnership with the principal.

Ending the Contract

Outsourcing is a contract, and contracts have a start date and an end date. Therefore, as with other contracts, it is imperative when embarking on it to do so with an idea of how to end it, too. Outsourcing contracts, and not necessarily IS ones, are ended because of three broad sets of reasons: (a) termination for cause, (b) termination for convenience, and (c) *force majeure*.[47] This applies to IS outsourcing contracts, too. *Termination for cause* happens when there is a material breach of the contract, such as the agent not delivering as required or when key personnel the agent promised in a time and materials contract are not there. Termination for a cause may also happen because the service is lousy or the price is no longer attractive. *Termination for convenience*, on the other hand, deals with cases where the principal or the agent decides to stop the contract without claiming that the other did not do what it was contracted to do. It is customary to provide adequate notice, such as a 6-month notice, in this case. *Force majeure* deals with cases beyond the reasonable control of either the principal or the agent that warrant stopping the contract. These may include cases such as floods that disable the disk farm. With a 50% failure rate in IS outsourcing projects,[48] it is unrealistic not to plan for and take precautions for possible failure.

Another reason IS outsourcing contracts come to an end, and these are the stories with a happy ending, is when the process was a success and the contract reached its end date without serious problems. Even in these cases, it is imperative when the contract is being drafted to think what comes next. IS outsourcing projects are begun knowing that either the IS management will be brought in-house when it is done or its maintenance will be outsourced in another contract. How to proceed to this next step is an integral part of drafting the contract.

Putting things into perspective, according to the TPI report,[49] companies that renegotiated their outsourcing contracts did so for many reasons but seldom because they were not satisfied with the process or outcome. Typically, outsourcing contracts were renegotiated because of a change in the scope of the requirements or business needs, pricing stopped being attractive, or the contract came to an end and had to be renewed. Often, when things went wrong it was because, while the principal invested a lot in setting up the process, it did not emphasize its continuous management or it lacked sufficient experience in managing the contract. IS outsourcing is a process; it requires more than just signing a contract properly. Other times projects failed, according to the TPI report, was because of unrealistic expectations on behalf of either the principal or the agent. And then, there were cases when the agent did not deliver.

Whatever the cause, breaking up is hard to do. One way of addressing this is to add an explicit clause in the contract dealing with terminating for a cause and how such material breach of contract should be dealt with legally, including when the principal does not need to pay termination fees. This is easier said than done when dealing with something more than a totally standardized service. In the case of IS development outsourcing, for example, is it very hard to prove that either party did not live up to its obligations. At any rate, if the matter ends up in court, it may take too long to resolve and may leave terrible PR problems for both sides, let alone the high transaction costs that may render the whole litigation process not worthwhile. Transaction costs in this case include not only legal fees but also the time needed to collect and organize all the material and the time invested in managing the trial.

In the case of terminating for convenience, which may occur, for example, when a new technology is made available so that a contract for outsourcing to use an older technology is no longer relevant, there should be in place a process for proper notification and paying a fine. Again, it is a matter of a long-term perspective that the principal wants to take to avoid creating for itself the name of a bad client, and with this bad PR discourage agents who can go elsewhere from bidding on its future contracts as well as causing those agents who do bid to bid higher than they might have otherwise on account of the increased risk with this principal. Nonetheless, there may be good reasons to terminate an outsourcing contract for convenience. These reasons include renegotiation with the objective of adding services to the current contract with the same agent because either the content of the specs has changed or the nature of available technology has changed. Another good reason is to renegotiate how the agent is supplying its current services, such as unifying several contracts into one, changing to SaaS, and adding or removing agent personnel.

At any rate, the contract should be signed in the first place realizing the outsourcing relationship will eventually end, and so the principal should insist that the agent and its personnel should sign a confidentiality and confidential disclosure agreement, including a noncompete clause.[50]

Capturing the Essence of Outsourcing

Outsourcing is a complex process, and for those who have little experience with it firsthand, things may seem rather straightforward about it. So, to bring the message home, here is a well-known joke about dentists that captures some of the essence of outsourcing risks.

A woman walks into a dentist's office and asks, "How much will it cost to extract a tooth?" "Well," says the dentist, "the standard price is $190." The woman looks at him and says, "Too expensive. Can you reduce the price?" The dentist looks at her and then says, "well, I can give you only one Novocain shot. It will hurt more, but I would only charge $140." "That is better," says the woman, "but can you go any cheaper?" The dentist is clearly unhappy about this but says, "I could give you no Novocain at all. It will hurt terribly, but I can cut the cost to $90." "Any cheaper?" says the woman. The dentist is now really distraught but says, "Well, I can use the tools my grandfather used and charge you only $40, but really I do not recommend this." "Any cheaper?" responds the woman. "No, sorry, that is the cheapest it can be legally done" answers the dentist. "Okay," says the woman, "please make an appointment for my husband."

If you laughed at this joke, then you missed something in this book. The woman is the analogous outsourcing agent and the husband is the principal. Remember the Novocain!

The famous words presumably said by Michael Corleone in *The Godfather Part II*, "Keep your friends close and your enemies closer," apply equally well to IS outsourcing. Be aware.

Notes

Chapter 1

1. As translated in Wikipedia: "So it is said that if you know your enemies and know yourself, you can win a thousand battles without a single loss. If you only know yourself, but not your opponent, you may win or may lose. If you know neither yourself nor your enemy, you will always endanger yourself." http://en.wikipedia.org/wiki/The_Art_of_War

2. In Europe IT is called information and communication technologies (ICT). Although often spoken of as if they are one and the same, IS and IT are actually not the same. IS are the information *systems*. These are the software systems that have become an inseparable part of how organizations are run. IT is the information *technology*, such as hardware and telecomm, upon which these IS software systems are run. Consequently, the decision on when to outsource will be different with each.

3. Feld and Stoddard (2004).

4. Lacity and Hirschheim (1993).

5. Rogers (1967).

6. As a sign of the risks in being a Cloud computing vendor and as a client in signing up for services with Cloud vendors, Lala.com shut down on March 31, 2010. It was probably a brilliant idea that came before its time.

7. Dubie (2010a).

8. Dominguez (2006).

9. Dominguez (2006).

10. Deloitte (2005).

11. Aspray et al. (2006).

12. Szajna (1994).

13. Bolton and Dewatripont (2005).

14. Gaudin (2003).

15. Dominguez (2006).

16. Overby (2003).

17. Talking about maintaining legacy systems is somewhat misleading. It often means adding new features to older systems—and correcting the ensuing glitches this creates. This is often hard programming and requires a lot of skill because these older systems are often written in what computer sciences call "structured" programming, rather than "object-oriented" programming, and so every change

made may affect other things outside the module being reprogrammed. Let alone that documentation may be lacking and that the people who wrote those programs may have long since retired. See Dubie (2009b).

18. Schneider (2008).

19. McAfee and Brynjolfsson (2008).

20. Carr (2003).

21. A review of open source operating systems is available at http://en.wikipedia.org/wiki/Comparison_of_open_source_operating_systems

22. CMMI, http://www.sei.cmu.edu/cmmi/

23. Gefen et al. (2006).

24. Aspray et al. (2006).

25. Carr (2003).

26. *The Economist* (2010a).

27. Gottschalk and Solli-Saether (2006).

28. Ranganathan and Outlay (2009).

29. Ashley (2008).

30. Beizer (1990).

31. For example, see Brandel (2004).

32. M. E. Porter (2008).

33. Gefen et al. (2008).

34. Gefen and Carmel (2008).

35. Bahli and Rivard (2003).

36. Kelly and Noonan (2007).

37. There is some rivalry of claims as to when computers were first used. On the American side of the Atlantic it is claimed that the ENIAC was the first electronic computer, used initially to build the hydrogen bomb (http://en.wikipedia.org/wiki/ENIAC) On the British side it is claimed that Alan Turing in Bletchley Park (where British intelligence broke the German Enigma code in World War II) had the first electronic computer (Singh [2001]).

38. Gefen et al. (2010).

39. Gefen et al. (2010).

40. http://www.msnbc.msn.com/id/20254745/

41. Smick (2008).

42. Friedman (2005).

43. http://en.wikipedia.org/wiki/Closing_milestones_of_the_Dow_Jones_Industrial_Average

44. Smick (2008).

45. Smick (2008).

46. Prasso (2010).

47. Smick (2008).

48. Huff et al. (2004).

49. Huff (2010).

50. Dominguez (2006).

51. Outsourcing as a business practice is really not that new, nor are the risks of its mismanagement. It was a common practice in the Roman Empire, and in many empires before it, to outsource tax collection. Since the tax collector would retain a percentage of the tax as his fee, and since there was no oversight, tax collectors took advantage of their position to become rich. The revolt of Boudicca and her Iceni tribe in Britain against Rome in AD 60–61 with its disastrous results was not the first time, nor the last, that outsourcing went wrong.

52. Dominguez (2006).

53. Dominguez (2006).

54. http://en.wikipedia.org/wiki/The_Art_of_War

55. Drucker (1988).

56. The fascinating story of the adage appears in http://en.wikipedia.org/wiki/Murphy%E2%80%99s_law

57. http://www.boeing.com/commercial/787family/

58. http://www.bloomberg.com/apps/news?pid=20601087&sid=aF6uWvMb9C08

59. http://www.rttsweb.com/outsourcing/statistics/

Chapter 2

1. Lacity and Willcocks (1998).

2. Beulen et al. (2006).

3. Beulen et al. (2006).

4. Banerjee and Duflo (2000); Ethiraj et al. (2005); Lichtenstein and McDonnell (2003).

5. Bajari and Tadelis (2001); Crocker and Reynolds (1993); Rogerson (1994).

6. http://en.wikipedia.org/wiki/Software_crisis

7. The *software crisis* is still around today. Recent industry reports (Jones, 2010) claim that, as of 2002, 60% of manufacturing companies found glitches in the software they bought, and that in another study of 13,000 development projects only about 85% of software defects were removed. Moreover, even when CMMI is used the software delivered still has many defects: only about 79% of the defects are removed in CMMI level 1, going up to 91% in CMMI level 3, and almost 97% in the highest CMMI level 5 (Jones 2010).

8. Gefen et al. (2008b).

9. http://www.payscale.com/research/US/Certification=Oracle_Certified_Professional_(OCP)_DBA/Hourly_Rate and http://web-site-builders.com/FixedBidContract.pdf

10. Keil et al. (2000).

11. Banerjee and Duflo (2000).

12. Ethiraj et al. (2005).

13. Gefen (1991).

14. http://www.nist.gov/index.html

15. Mell and Grance (2009).

16. http://www.agilysys.com/home

17. http://en.wikipedia.org/wiki/Server_farm

18. Claburn (2008); Kanaracus (2010).

19. Mell and Grance (2009).

20. Conry-Murray (2010).

21. Murphy (2010).

22. Schneider (2010b).

23. Gefen et al. (2010).

24. Schneider (2010b).

25. Feldman (2010).

26. Carr (2003).

27. Feldman (2010).

28. Claburn (2008).

29. http://www.amadeus.com/airlineIT/solutions/sol_1altea_5customer_1departure.html

30. Carr (2003).

31. http://www.itnews.com.au/News/155428,ibm-qantas-ink-seven-year-outsourcing-deal.aspx; http://www.itnews.com.au/News/143762,fujitsu-usurps-telstra-at-qantas.aspx

32. Christensen (1997).

33. http://newsroom.elan.com/phoenix.zhtml?c=88326&p=irol-newsArticle&ID=1396368&highlight=

34. Aspray et al. (2006).

35. The academic world in most advanced countries is so integrated that chances are that many of these engineers, even if they studied in their own country, probably studied from the same American textbooks as American students do and even studied with professors who either received their degrees from American universities or did a post-doc there. Academic quality is not an issue. English proficiency in many cases is not an issue either because English, or to be exact American English, is the lingua franca of the business world.

36. http://www.payscale.com/research/IN/Years_Experience=10-19_years/Salary

37. Aspray et al. (2006).

38. Aspray et al. (2006).

39. Carmel et al. (2008).

40. http://en.wikipedia.org/wiki/North_American_Free_Trade_Agreement

41. Friedman (2005).

42. *The Economist* (2010b).

43. Senor and Singer (2010).

44. Frohman (2006).

45. http://errancarmel.blogspot.com/2008/07/micro-sourcing.html

46. Gefen et al. (2008b).

47. Gefen et al. (2008b).

48. http://www.theaustralian.com.au/news/qantas-cuts-750m-desktop-deal/story-e6frgal6-1225699958653

49. http://www.builderau.com.au/news/soa/Qantas-finalises-IBM-outsourcing-deal/0,339028227,339298430,00.htm

50. Beulen et al. (2006).

51. Gefen et al. (2008b).

52. Gefen and Carmel (2008).

53. Lichtenstein et al. (2010).

Chapter 3

1. You can read the whole book at http://etext.lib.virginia.edu/etcbin/toccer-new2?id=CarGlas.sgm&images=images/modeng&data=/texts/english/modeng/parsed&tag=public&part=2&division=div1

2. Ashley (2008).

3. Rogers (1967).

4. Carr (2003).

5. http://en.wikipedia.org/wiki/Cobol

6. http://en.wikipedia.org/wiki/NAICS

7. The figures are copied here with permission from Baldwin. The originals appear at http://www.people.hbs.edu/cbaldwin/DR2/BaldwinDesignTheoryAndMethods2007.ppt

8. Jetter (2009).

9. Schneider (2010a).

10. http://en.wikipedia.org/wiki/Moore%27s_law

11. http://en.wikipedia.org/wiki/Electronic_Data_Interchange

12. Currie and Seltsikas (2001).

13. Carr (2003).

14. Rogers (1967).

15. A summary of the theory is available at http://en.wikipedia.org/wiki/Diffusion_of_innovations. In essence, Rogers presents the progression of a new innovation as though it occurs on a bell-shape graph where it goes through five discrete stages separated by vertical lines. The first stage involves the innovators who are drawn in the extreme left 2.5% of the graph, followed to their right by the early adopters taking up another 13.5%, and then to their right the early majority take up another 34%. To the right of the early majority, the late majority takes up another 34%, followed by the laggards who make up the remaining 16%. Although not part of the graph, there is a conceptual mind shift, a psychological barrier, between the innovators and the early adopters and between the early adopters and the early majority.

16. Moore (1991).
17. Moore (1991).
18. Moore (1991).
19. Moore (1991).
20. Moore (1991).
21. Hammer and Champy (1993).
22. Moore (1991).
23. Rogers (1967).
24. Carr (2003).
25. http://www.nist.gov/index.html
26. Babcock (2010).
27. M. E. Porter (1979).
28. http://elan2006.blogspot.com/2008/07/elan-wyeth-study-finds-alzheimers
-drug.html
29. Phase 3 testing means the drug is being administered to patients in an experimental and controlled manner. This is the last phase before potential approval by the FDA. At this stage the drug has already passed the regulatory requirements of the FDA of Phase 1, which establishes its safety on healthy humans by showing their tolerance to the drug, and of Phase 2, which is small-scale clinical testing to show its effectiveness on real patients. http://en.wikipedia
.org/wiki/Regulatory_requirement
30. In fact, Salk put the vaccine in the public domain as a gift to humanity. There is no patent on the vaccine; it was never about money. http://en.wikipedia
.org/wiki/Jonas_Salk
31. Carr (2003).
32. McAfee (2006).
33. Carr (2003).
34. Schrage (2003).
35. Carr (2003).
36. Currie and Seltsikis (2001).
37. McAfee (2006).
38. Carr (2003).
39. Carr (2003).
40. Carr (2003).
41. Carr (2003).
42. Christensen (1997).

Chapter 4

1. Healey (2010).
2. Carr (2003).
3. Healey (2010).

4. Eisenhardt (1989).

5. Bolton and Dewatripont (2005).

6. Donaldson (1990); Jensen and Meckling (1976).

7. Mishra et al. (1998).

8. Hsieh (2010), p. 42.

9. For example, Aubert et al. (2005); Kalnins and Mayer (2004), and Snir and Hitt (2004).

10. McDougall (2006).

11. Gefen et al. (2008b).

12. Gefen et al. (2008b).

13. Gopal et al. (2003).

14. Gefen (2004).

15. Gefen et al. (2008b); Kumar (1996); Rai et al. (2009); Rustagi et al. (2008).

16. A fascinating list of such glitches is available at http://web.nvd.nist.gov/view/vuln/statistics

17. Drucker (1988).

18. http://zapatopi.net/kelvin/quotes/

19. Rai et al. (2009).

20. Gefen (2002); Ragowsky and Gefen (2009).

21. Tiwana and Keil (2009).

22. Rai et al. (2009).

23. Gefen et al. (2008b).

24. Gulati (1995).

25. Gefen et al. (2008b); Kumar et al. (1995).

26. Kalnins and Mayer (2004).

27. Lander et al. (2004).

28. Gefen et al. (2008b).

29. Corts and Singh (2004).

30. Gonzalez et al. (2006).

31. Gulati (1995); Kumar et al. (1995).

32. Gefen et al. (2008b).

33. Halstead (1977).

34. Gefen (1995).

35. SCADA is the ability to control industrial IS such as manufacturing and electric grid control remotely.

36. Bolton and Dewatripont (2005).

37. Gefen et al. (2008b).

38. Feld and Stoddard (2004).

39. Benaroch et al. (2007); Lichtenstein et al. (2010).

40. People are cognitively challenged: none of us is as clever as we would like. So, if something cannot be made simple, there is probably something we do not understand in the process.

41. Rustagi et al. (2008).

42. In *Letters written by the late right honourable Philip Dormer Stanhope, Earl of Chesterfield, to his son Philip Stanhope esq.* (1753, December 25), http://www.rhul.ac.uk/Classics/CUCD/atkins.html

43. Markus (1983).

44. Kelly and Noonan (2007).

45. Lichtenstein et al. (2010).

46. Bolton and Dewatripont (2005).

47. Gefen et al. (2008b).

48. Beizer (1990). The 2.7 bugs per KLOC was based on an average of a host of large software projects. In projects I managed (e.g., Gefen, 1991) the numbers came out almost the same.

49. Levina and Ross (2003).

50. Gefen et al. (2008b); Kalnins and Mayer (2004).

51. Gefen and Carmel (2008).

52. These are methodologies for tracking the progress of projects and specifically how milestones relate to each other over time. In some versions the progression of the milestones is associated with personnel and resources.

53. Gefen (2002, 2004); Gefen et al. (2008b); Goo et al. (2009); Rai et al. (2009); Scott (2000); Son et al. (2005).

54. Dinev and Hart (2006); Levin and Cross (2004); Nelson and Cooprider (1996); Porter and Donthu (2008); Scott (2000).

55. Ågerfalk and Fitzgerald (2008); Ganesan (1994); Gefen (2004); Gefen et al. (2008b); Goo et al. (2009); Kumar (1996); Rai et al. (2009); Rustagi et al. (2008); Son et al. (2005).

56. Gefen (2002).

57. McAfee (2006), p. 142.

58. Gefen and Ridings (2003).

59. In theoretical terms this is called *social identification theory.* This theory was created by Tajfel (1970, 1978) and expanded by Turner (1985), Deaux (1996), and Hogg and Terry (2000). In a nutshell, people think more highly of others they think are associated with them, the in-group, than they do of strangers, the out-group. Moreover, people will exaggerate, or even make up, the similarities between them and the in-group and the differences between themselves and the out-group. As part of this process of self-identification, people will also adopt what they think are the values and beliefs of their in-group—which could be very important in the case of managing IS adoption because managers can increase the adoption of new IS by reducing the tension between the in-group the users think they belong to and the IS out-group (Gefen & Ridings, 2003).

60. Lichtenstein et al. (2010).

61. Ashley (2008).

62. Ashley (2008).

63. Rai et al. (2009).

64. Ashley (2008).

65. Gefen et al. (2008b).

66. Beizer (1990).

67. Lichtenstein et al. (2010).

68. Ashley (2008).

69. Deloitte (2005).

70. Schneider (2008).

71. Mehling (2010).

72. Gopal and Sivaramakrishnan (2008).

73. Mehling (2010).

74. Lemon (2010).

75. Lacity and Hirschheim (1993).

76. Beulen et al. (2006).

77. Ang and Straub (1998).

Chapter 5

1. http://www.kipling.org.uk/poems_normansaxon.htm

2. Watjatrakul (2005).

3. Eisenhardt (1989).

4. Buehler et al. (2008).

5. Barki et al. (1993, 2001).

6. Mumford and Henshall (1978).

7. Some interesting additions to this literature include Matta and Ashkenas (2003) and Feld and Stoddard (2004).

8. Barki et al. (1993, 2001).

9. Markus (1983).

10. Barki and Hartwick (2001); Igbaria and Maragahh (1995).

11. Boland (1978); Robey and Farrow (1982); Salaway (1987).

12. Hunton and Beeler (1997); Hunton and Price (1997).

13. Hartwick and Barki (2001).

14. Gefen et al. (2008a).

15. Bies and Moag (1986); Tyler (1989).

16. Cropanzano et al. (2002); Greenberg (1990).

17. McColl-Kennedy and Sparks (2003).

18. Colquitt et al. (2001).

19. Leung et al. (2004).

20. Skarlicki and Folger (1997).

21. Gefen et al. (2008a).

22. Ignatius (2010).

23. Gefen et al. (2008b); Rai et al. (2009).

24. Kanter (2003).

25. Gefen et al. (2010).

26. Ragowsky and Gefen (2009).

27. Feld and Stoddard (2004).

28. Pavlou and Gefen (2005).

29. Morrison and Robinson (1997); Niehoff and Paul (2001); Pate and Malone (2000); Pugh et al. (2003); Robinson (1996); Rousseau (1989).

30. Pugh et al. (2003).

31. Kanter (2003).

32. Pavlou and Gefen (2005).

33. Dimoka (2010).

34. Joshi (1991); Lamertz (2002); Leung et al. (2004); Skarlicki and Folger (1997); Tyler (1989).

35. Hammer and Champy (2003).

36. Ragowsky and Gefen (2009).

37. Markus (1983).

38. Levinson (2010).

39. Hammer and Champy (1993).

40. Norman et al. (2010).

41. Gefen (2002).

42. Nayar (2010).

43. Ashley (2008).

44. Tay (2009).

45. IBM (2002).

46. Drucker (1988).

47. Janis (1983).

48. Joni and Beyer (2009).

49. Joni and Beyer (2009).

50. Tay (2009).

51. Hammer and Champy (2003).

52. Feld and Stoddard (2004).

53. Feld and Stoddard (2004).

54. Matta and Ashkenas (2003).

55. For example, Lichtenstein et al. (2010).

56. Ottenstein (1979).

57. Gefen (1991).

58. Beulen et al. (2006).

59. Matta and Ashkenas (2003).

60. Gefen et al. (2010).

61. Buehler et al. (2008).

62. Gefen et al. (2010).

63. Rogers (1967).

64. Szajna (1994).
65. Gaudin (2003).
66. Deloitte (2005).
67. Deloitte (2005).
68. Bolton and Dewatripont (2005).
69. Gefen et al. (2010).
70. Ashley (2008).
71. Deloitte (2005).
72. Mehling (2010).
73. Matta and Ashkenas (2003).
74. Feld and Stoddard (2004).
75. Feld and Stoddard (2004).
76. Gottschalk and Solli-Saether (2006)
77. Carr (2003).
78. Gottschalk and Solli-Saether (2006).
79. Gottschalk and Solli-Saether (2006).
80. Gottschalk and Solli-Saether (2006).
81. http://www-03.ibm.com/press/us/en/pressrelease/27936.wss
82. Gottschalk and Solli-Saether (2006).
83. Ragowsky et al. (2008).
84. Williamson (1979).
85. Williamson (1985).
86. Malone and Laubacher (1998).
87. Watjatrakul (2005).
88. Schneider (2010b).

Chapter 6

1. http://www.kipling.org.uk/poems_normansaxon.htm
2. Feld and Stoddard (2004).
3. Gefen et al. (2008b).
4. Matta and Ashkenas (2003).
5. Lichtenstein et al. (2010).
6. As translated in http://academic.brooklyn.cuny.edu/core9/phalsall/texts/suntzu.html
7. Ragowsky and Gefen (2009).
8. Feld and Stoddard (2004).
9. Beulen et al. (2006).
10. Beulen et al. (2006).
11. Beulen et al. (2006).
12. Beulen et al. (2006).
13. Chapman (2009).

14. Gopal and Sivaramakrishnan (2008).

15. http://en.wikipedia.org/wiki/Semi_Automatic_Ground_Environment

16. http://en.wikipedia.org/wiki/Sabre_(computer_system)

17. http://www.computerworld.com/action/article.do?command=viewArticle Basic&articleId=9126879 and http://www.daniweb.com/blogs/entry1466.html

18. http://www.computerworld.com/managementtopics/outsourcing/story/ 0,10801,97450,00.html

19. Gefen et al. (2008b).

20. Gefen et al. (2010).

21. Carr (2003).

22. Williamson (1985).

23. Bolton and Dewatripont (2005).

24. Bolton and Dewatripont (2005).

25. https://www.fbo.gov/index?mode=list&s=opportunity

26. Gefen and Carmel (2008).

27. Gefen and Carmel (2010).

28. Gopal et al. (2003).

29. Whang (1995).

30. Gefen (2002).

31. Gefen (2002).

32. Gefen (2004).

33. Beulen et al. (2006).

34. Gefen et al. (2008a).

35. http://www.outsourcing-transition-management.com/failures.html

36. Feeny et al. (2005).

37. Koh and Ang (2008).

38. Koh and Ang (2008).

39. Ashley (2008); Koh and Ang (2008).

40. Rustagi et al. (2008).

41. Rustagi et al. (2008).

42. Gefen et al. (2008b).

43. Coming from the agent side, I would add that the same applies to the agent who should specify in the contract exactly what it expects of the principal, although it is not always politically possible to be as blunt when you are the agent.

44. Kanter (2003).

45. Kanter (2003).

46. Beulen et al. (2006).

47. Ashley (2008).

48. Gaudin (2003).

49. http://www.tpi.net/

50. Examples of such can be found at http://www.ipo.gov.uk/cda.pdf

References

Ågerfalk, P. J., & Fitzgerald, B. (2008). Outsourcing to an unknown workforce: Exploring Opensourcing as a global sourcing strategy. *MIS Quarterly, 32*(2), 385–409.

Ang, S., & Straub, D. W. (1998). Production and transaction economies and IS outsourcing: A study of the U.S. banking industry. *MIS Quarterly, 22*(4), 535–552.

Ashley, E. (2008). *Outsourcing for dummies.* New York, NY: Wiley.

Aspray, W., Mayadas, F., & Vardi, M. Y. (2006). Globalization and Offshoring of Software. A Report of the ACM Job Migration Task Force. Retrieved from http://www.acm.org/globalizationreport

Aubert, B. A., Patry, M., & Rivard, S. (2005). A framework for information technology outsourcing risk management. *Database for Advances in Information Systems, 36*(4), 9–28.

Babcock, C. (2010, July 27). Cloud Working Group Developing Standard APIs. *InformationWeek.* Retrieved from http://www.informationweek.com/news/storage/virtualization/showArticle.jhtml?articleID=226200299&cid=nl_IW_cloud_2010-07-28_h

Bahli, B., & Rivard, S. (2003). The information technology outsourcing risk: A transaction cost and agency theory-based perspective. *Journal of Information Technology, 18*, 211–221.

Bajari, P., & Tadelis, S. (2001). Incentives versus transaction costs: A theory of procurement contracts. *RAND Journal of Economics, 32*(3), 387–407.

Banerjee, A., & Duflo, E. (2000). Reputation effects and the limits of contracting: A study of the Indian software industry. *Quarterly Journal of Economics, 115*(3), 989–1017.

Barki, H., & Hartwick, J. (2001). Interpersonal conflict and its management in information system development. *MIS Quarterly, 25*(2), 195–228.

Barki, H., Rivard, S., & Talbot, J. (1993). Toward an assessment of software development risk. *Journal of Management Information Systems, 10*(2), 203–225.

Barki, H., Rivard, S., & Talbot, J. (2001). An integrative contingency model of software project risk management. *Journal of Management Information Systems, 17*(4), 37–69.

Beizer, B. (1990). *Software systems techniques.* New York, NY: Van Nostrand Reinhold.

Benaroch, M., Jeffery, M., Kauffman, R. J., & Shah, S. (2007). Option-based risk management: A field study of sequential information technology investment decisions. *Journal of Management Information Systems, 24*(2), 103–140.

Beulen, E., Ribbers, P., & Roos, J. (2006). *Managing IT outsourcing: Governance in global partnerships*. London, England: Routledge, Taylor & Francis Group.

Bies, R., & Moag, J. (1986). Interactional justice: Communication criteria of fairness. In R. Lewicki, M. Bazerman, & B. Sheppard (Eds.), *Research on negotiation in organizations* (pp. 43–55). Greenwich, CT: JAI Press.

Boland, R. J. (1978). The process and product of systems design. *Management Science, 24*(9), 887–898.

Bolton, P., & Dewatripont, M. (2005). *Contract theory*. Cambridge, MA: MIT Press.

Brandel, M. (2004, November 15). Sinking quality. Prevent contractor performance from slipping after the honeymoon is over. *Computerworld*. Retrieved from http://www.computerworld.com/s/article/97450/Sinking_Quality?taxonomyId=060

Buehler, K., Freeman, A., & Hulme, R. (2008). Owning the right risks. *Harvard Business Review, 86*(9), 102–110.

Carmel, E., Gao, G., & Zhang, N. (2008). The maturing Chinese offshore IT services industry: It takes 10 years to sharpen a sword. *MISQe, 7*(4), 157–170.

Carr, N. G. (2003). IT doesn't matter. *Harvard Business Review, 81*(5), 41–49.

Chapman, S. (2009, June 16). Gartner: Don't sign long-term outsourcing deals. *NetworkWorld*. Retrieved from http://www.networkworld.com/news/2009/061609-gartner-dont-sign-long-term-outsourcing.html

Christensen, C. M. (1997). *The innovator's dilemma*. Boston, MA: Harvard Business School Press.

Claburn, T. (2008, October 15). Cloud summit: SAP sees bright future in Cloud computing. *InformationWeek*. Retrieved from http://www.informationweek.com/news/services/business/showArticle.jhtml?articleID=211200756

Clark, J. G., Warren, J., & Au, Y. A. (2009). Assessing researcher publication productivity in the leading information systems journals: A 2003–2007 update. *Communications of the Association for Information Systems, 24*(14), 225–254.

Colquitt, J. A., Conlon, D. E., Wesson, M. J., Porter, C. O. L. H., & Ng, K. Y. (2001). Justice at the millennium: A meta-analytic review of 25 years of organizational justice research. *Journal of Applied Psychology, 86*(3), 425–445.

Conry-Murray, A. (2010, April 26). SaaS e-mail's moment. *InformationWeek.com*, pp. 19–24.

Corts, K. S., & Singh, J. (2004). The effect of repeated interaction on contract choice: Evidence from offshore drilling. *Journal of Law Economics & Organization, 20*(1), 230–260.

Crocker, K. J., & Reynolds, R. J. (1993). The efficiency of incomplete contracts: An empirical analysis of air force engine procurement. *RAND Journal of Economics, 24*, 126–146.

Cropanzano, R., Prehar, C. A., & Chen, P. Y. (2002). Using social exchange theory to distinguish procedural from interactional justice. *Group & Organization Management, 27*(3), 324–351.

Currie, W. L., & Seltsikas, P. (2001). Exploring the supply-side of IT outsourcing: Evaluating the emerging role of application service providers. *European Journal of Information Systems, 10*, 123–134.

Deaux, K. (1996). Social identification. In E. T. Higgins & A. W. Kruglanski (Eds.), *Social psychology handbook of basic principles* (pp. 777–798). New York, NY, and London, England: Guilford Press.

Deloitte. (2005). Calling a change in outsourcing market. The realities of the world's largest organizations. Retrieved from http://www.deloitte.com/dtt/cda/doc/content/us_outsourcing_callingachange.pdf

Dimoka, A. (2010). What does our brain tell us about trust and distrust? Evidence from a nunctional Neuroimaging study. *MIS Quarterly, 34*(2), 373–396.

Dinev, T., & Hart, P. (2006). An extended privacy calculus model for e-commerce transactions. *Information Systems Research, 17*(1), 61–80.

Dominguez, L. R. (2006). *The manager's step-by-step guide to outsourcing.* New York, NY: McGraw-Hill.

Donaldson, L. (1990). The ethereal hand: Organizational economics and management theory. *Academy of Management Review, 15*(3), 369–381.

Drucker, P. F. (1988). The coming of the new organization. *Harvard Business Review, 66*(1), 45–53.

Dubie, D. (2009a). Economy could break outsourcers, analysts say. *Computerworld.* Retrieved from http://www.computerworld.com/s/article/9134462/Economy_could_break_outsourcers_analysts_say?source=CTWNLE_nlt_dailyam_2009-06-17

Dubie, D. (2009b). IT staff cuts top list of budget reduction plans. *Computerworld.* Retrieved from http://www.computerworld.com/s/article/9136928/IT_staff_cuts_top_list_of_budget_reduction_plans?source=CTWNLE_nlt_dailyam_2009-08-21

Economist. (2010a, July 24–30). Banking and IT: Compter says no. *The Economist,* p. 74.

Economist. (2010b, March 13–19). Older and wiser: A special report on Germany. *The Economist,* pp. 1–16.

Eisenhardt, K. M. (1989). Agency theory: An assessment and review. *Academy of Management Review, 14*(1), 57–74.

Ethiraj, S. K., Kale, P., Krishnan, M. S., & Singh, J. V. (2005). Where do capabilities come from and how do they matter? A study in the software services industry. *Strategic Management Journal, 26*(1), 25–45.

Feeny, D., Lacity, M., & Willcocks, L. P. (2005). Taking the measure of outsourcing providers. *MIT Sloan Management Review, 46*(3), 41–48.

Feld, C. S., & Stoddard, D. B. (2004). Getting IT right. *Harvard Business Review, 82*(2), 72–79.

Feldman, J. (2010, June 21). Could ROI: A grounded view. *InformationWeek* (1,271), 39–40.

Friedman, T. L. (2005). *The world is flat: A brief history of the twenty-first century.* New York, NY: Farrar, Straus and Giroux.

Frohman, D. (2006). Leadership under fire. *Harvard Business Review, 84*(12), 124–131.

Ganesan, S. (1994). Determinants of long-term orientation in buyer-seller relationships. *Journal of Marketing, 58*(1), 1–19.

Gaudin, S. (2003, November 25). Choosing the right country for IT offshoring. *Datamation.* Retrieved from http://itmanagement.earthweb.com/erp/article.php/3113491/Choosing-the-Right-Country-for-IT-Offshoring.htm

Gefen, D. (1991). *Software errors in application development using an application generator: An empirical study of their frequency and distribution.* Unpublished master's thesis, Tel-Aviv University, Tel-Aviv, Israel.

Gefen, D. (1995). *Analysis errors' estimation in a large MIS: Two empirical case studies.* Paper presented at the 13th Annual Pacific Northwest Software Quality Conference, Portland, Oregon.

Gefen, D. (2002). Nurturing clients' trust to encourage engagement success during the customization of ERP systems. *Omega: The International Journal of Management Science, 30*(4), 287–299.

Gefen, D. (2004). What makes ERP implementation relationships worthwhile: Linking Trust mechanisms and ERP usefulness. *Journal of Management Information Systems, 23*(1), 263–288.

Gefen, D., & Carmel, E. (2008). Is the world really flat? A look at offshoring in an online programming marketplace. *MIS Quarterly, 32*(2), 367–384.

Gefen, D., & Carmel, E. (2010). *Determinants of project success in online software marketplaces: Thresholds and what ratings really predict.* Working paper.

Gefen, D., Ragowsky, A., Licker, P., & Stern, M. (2010). *The changing role of the CIO in the world of outsourcing: Lessons learnt from a CIO roundtable.* Unpublished manuscript.

Gefen, D., Ragowsky, A., & Ridings, C. M. (2008a). Leadership and justice: Increasing non-participating users' assessment of an IT through passive participation. *Information & Management, 45*, 507–512.

Gefen, D., & Ridings, C. M. (2003). IT acceptance: Managing user–IT group boundaries. *The DATA BASE for Advances in Information Systems, 34*(3), 25–40.

Gefen, D., Wyss, S., & Lichtenstein, Y. (2008b). Business familiarity as risk mitigation in software development outsourcing contracts. *MIS Quarterly, 32*(3), 531–551.

Gefen, D., Zviran, M., & Elman, N. (2006). What can be learned from failed CMMi projects? *Communications of the Association for Information Systems, 17*(36), 801–817.

Gonzalez, R., Gascoa, J., & Llopisa, J. (2006). Information systems offshore outsourcing: A descriptive analysis. *Industrial Management + Data Systems, 106*(9), 1233–1248.

Goo, J., Kishore, R., Rao, H. R., & Nam, K. (2009). The role of service level agreements in relational management of information technology outsourcing: An empirical study. *MIS Quarterly, 33*(1), 119–145.

Gopal, A., & Sivaramakrishnan, K. (2008). On vendor preference for contract types in offshore software projects: The case of fixed price vs. time and materials contracts. *Information Systems Research, 19*(2), 202–220.

Gopal, A., Sivaramakrishnan, K., Krishnan, M. S., & Mukhopadhyay, T. (2003). Contracts in offshore software development: An empirical analysis. *Management Science, 49*(12), 1671–1683.

Gottschalk, P., & Solli-Saether, H. (2006). Maturity model for IT outsourcing relationships. *Industrial Management + Data Systems, 106*(1/2), 200–212.

Greenberg, J. (1990). Organizational justice: Yesterday, today, and tomorrow. *Journal of Management, 16*(2), 399–432.

Gulati, R. (1995). Does familiarity breed trust? The implications of repeated ties for contractual choice in alliances. *Academy of Management Journal, 38*(1), 85–112.

Halstead, M. H. (1977). *Elements of software science.* New York, NY: Elsevier Science.

Hammer, M., & Champy, J. (1993). *Reengineering the corporation.* New York, NY: Harper Business.

Hammer, M., & Champy, J. (2003). *Reengineering the corporation: A manifesto for business revolution.* New York, NY: Harper Paperbacks.

Hartwick, J., & Barki, H. (2001). Communication as a dimension of user participation. *IEEE Transactions on Professional Communication, 44*(1), 21–36.

Healey, M. (2010, April 10). Outsourcing. *Information Week,* 17–27. Retrieved from http://www.informationweek.com/gogreen/041910/download.jhtml;jsessionid =4DBQRP3VBGK5VQE1GHRSKH4ATMY32JVN?_requestid=75590

Hogg, M. A., & Terry, D. J. (2000). Social identity and self-categorization processes in organizational contexts. *Academy of Management Review, 25*(1), 121–140.

Hsieh, T. (2010). Zappos's CEO on going to extremes for customers. *Harvard Business Review, 88*(7/8), 41–45.

Huff, S. L., Maher, M. P., & Munro, M. C. (2004, September–October). What boards don't know—but must do—about information technology. *Ivey Business Journal*, pp. 1–4.

Hunton, J. E., & Beeler, J. D. (1997). Effects of user participation in systems development: A longitudinal field experiment. *MIS Quarterly, 21*(4), 359–388.

Hunton, J. E., & Price, K. H. (1997). Effects of the user participation process and task meaningfulness on key information system outcomes. *Management Science, 43*(6), 797–813.

IBM. (2002, November 12). DBS Bank and IBM announce an IT services initiative. *IBM*. Retrieved from http://www-03.ibm.com/press/us/en/pressrelease/435.wss

Igbaria, M. I., & Maragahh, H. J. (1995). Why do individuals use computer technology? A Finnish case study. *Information & Management, 29*(5), 227–238.

Ignatius, A. (2010). We had to own the mistakes. *Harvard Business Review, 88*(7/8), 109–115.

Janis, I. L. (1983). *Groupthink: Psychological studies of policy decisions and fiascoes.* Boston, MA: Houghton Mifflin.

Jensen, M., & Meckling, W. (1976). Theory of the firm: Managerial behavior, agency costs, and ownership structure. *Journal of Financial Economics, 3*(4), 305–360.

Jetter, M. (2009). Technological innovation and its impact on business model, organization and corporate culture—IBM`s transformation into a globally integrated, service-oriented enterprise. *Business & Information Systems Engineering, 1*, 37–45.

Jones, C. (2010, June 28). Get software quality right. *InformationWeek* (1,272), 25–32.

Joni, S.-n. A., & Beyer, D. (2009). How to pick a good fight. *Harvard Business Review, 87*(12), 48–57.

Joshi, K. (1991). A model of users' perspective on change: The case of information systems technology implementation. *MIS Quarterly, 15*(2), 229–242.

Kalnins, A., & Mayer, K. J. (2004). Relationships and hybrid contracts: An analysis of contract choice in information technology. *Journal of Law Economics and Organization, 20*(1), 207–229.

Kanaracus, C. (2010). SAP set to unveil first app for new 'River' Cloud platform. *Computerworld*. Retrieved from http://www.computerworld.com/s/article/9178636/SAP_set_to_unveil_first_app_for_new_River_cloud_platform?source=CTWNLE_nlt_pm_2010-06-28

Kanter, R. M. (2003). Leadership and the psychology of turnaround. *Harvard Business Review, 81*(6), 58–67.

Keil, M., Mann, J., & Rai, A. (2000). Why software projects escalate: An empirical analysis and test of four theoretical models. *MIS Quarterly, 24*(4), 631–664.

Kelly, S., & Noonan, C. (2007, December). *Producing comfort: Risk, anxiety and trust in the development of an IS offshoring relationship.* Paper presented at the 28th International Conference on Information Systems, Montreal, Quebec, Canada.

Koh, C., & Ang, S. (2008). Contracting in IT outsourcing. In S. Rivard & B. A. Aubert (Eds.), *Advances in management information systems* (pp. 289–304). Armonk, NY: M. E. Sharpe.

Kumar, N. (1996). The power of trust in manufacturer-retailer relationships. *Harvard Business Review, 74*(6), 92–106.

Kumar, N., Scheer, L. K., & Steenkamp, J.-B. E. M. (1995, February). The effects of supplier fairness on vulnerable resellers. *Journal of Marketing Research, 17*, 54–65.

Lacity, M. C., & Hirschheim, R. (1993, Fall). The information systems outsourcing bandwagon. *Sloan Management Review, 35*, 73–86.

Lacity, M. C., & Willcocks, L. P. (1998). An empirical investigation of information technology sourcing practices: Lessons from experience. *MIS Quarterly, 22*(3), 363–408.

Lamertz, K. (2002). The social construction of fairness: Social influence and sense making in organizations. *Journal of Organizational Behavior, 23*(1), 19–37.

Lander, M. C., Purvis, R. L., & McCray, G. E. (2004). Trust-building mechanisms utilized in outsourced IS development projects: A case study. *Information & Management, 41*, 509–528.

Lemon, S. (2010, July 13). IBM takes blame for massive bank system failure. *Computerworld.* Retrieved from http://www.computerworld.com/s/article/9179121/IBM_takes_blame_for_massive_bank_system_failure?source=CTWNLE_nlt_pm_2010-07-13

Leung, K., Tong, K.-K., & Ho, S. S.-Y. (2004). Effects of interactional justice on egocentric bias in resource allocation decisions. *Journal of Applied Psychology, 89*(3), 405–415.

Levin, D. Z., & Cross, R. (2004). The strength of weak ties you can trust: The mediating role of trust in effective knowledge transfer. *Management Science, 50*(11), 1477–1490.

Levina, N., & Ross, J. W. (2003). From the vendor's perspective: Exploring the value proposition in information technology outsourcing. *MIS Quarterly, 27*(3), 331–364.

Levinson, M. (2010, July 14). 10 communication mistakes CIOs still make. *CIO Magazine.* Retrieved from http://www.cio.com/article/599475/10 _Communication_Mistakes_CIOs_Still_Make

Lichtenstein, Y., Gefen, D., & Wyss, S. (2010). It is really not only about costs: The tacit advantage of local vendors—Three perspectives on international trade in software development services. *SSRN,* 1–11. Retrieved from http:// papers.ssrn.com/sol3/cf_dev/AbsByAuth.cfm?per_id=410198#

Lichtenstein, Y., & McDonnell, A. (2003, June 16–21). *Pricing software development services.* Paper presented at the 11th European Conference on Information Systems, Naples, Italy.

Malone, T. W., & Laubacher, R. J. (1998, September–October). The dawn of the e-lance economy. *Harvard Business Review, 76*(5), 145–152.

Markus, M. L. (1983). Power, politics, and MIS implementation. *Communication of the ACM, 26*(6), 430–444.

Matta, N. F., & Ashkenas, R. N. (2003). Why good projects fail anyway. *Harvard Business Review, 81*(9), 109–114.

McAfee, A. (2006). Mastering the three worlds of information technology. *Harvard Business Review, 84*(11), 141–149.

McAfee, A., & Brynjolfsson, E. (2008). Investing in the IT that makes a competitive difference. *Harvard Business Review, 86*(7/8), 98–107.

McColl-Kennedy, J., & Sparks, B. A. (2003). Application of fairness theory to service failures and service recovery. *Journal of Service Research, 5*(3), 251–266.

McDougall, P. (2006, June 19). Dexterity required. *InformationWeek*, pp. 34–39.

Mehling, H. (2010). Survey: Most software bugs due to poor testing procedures. When a bug is found in released software, the bottom-line impact on an organization is significant. Devx.com. Retrieved from http://www.devx.com/ enterprise/Article/45005

Mell, P., & Grance, T. (2009). The NIST definition of Cloud computing. Retrieved from http://csrc.nist.gov/groups/SNS/cloud-computing/

Mishra, D. P., Heide, J. B., & Cort, S. G. (1998). Information asymmetry and levels of agency relationships. *Journal of Marketing Research, 35*, 277–295.

Moore, G. A. (1991). *Crossing the chasm.* New York, NY: Harper Business Essentials.

Morrison, E. W., & Robinson, S. L. (1997). When employees feel betrayed: A model of how psychological contract violation develops. *Academy of Management Review, 22*, 226–256.

Mumford, E., & Henshall, D. (1978). *Participative approach to the design of computer systems.* London, England: Associated Business Press.

Murphy, C. (2010, May 3). Microsoft's Cloud plan. *InformationWeek*, pp. 29–34.

Nayar, V. (2010). A maverick CEO explains how he persuaded his team to leap into the future. *Harvard Business Review, 88*(6), 110–113.

Nelson, K. M., & Cooprider, J. G. (1996). The contribution of shared knowledge to IS group performance. *MIS Quarterly, 20*(4), 409–429.

Niehoff, B. P., & Paul, R. J. (2001). The just workplace: Developing and maintaining effective psychological contracts. *Review of Business, 22*(1/2), 5–8.

Norman, S. M., Avolio, B. J., & Luthans, F. (2010). The impact of positivity and transparency on trust in leaders and their perceived effectiveness. *Leadership Quarterly, 21*(3), 350–364.

Ottenstein, L. M. (1979). Quantitative estimates of debugging requirements. *IEEE Transactions on Software Engineering, 5*(5), 504–514.

Overby, S. (2003, March 1). Outsourcing: Bringing IT back home. *CIO*. Retrieved from http://www.cio.com/article/31733/Outsourcing_Bringing_IT_Back _Home?page=1&taxonomyId=3195

Pate, J., & Malone, C. (2000). Enduring perceptions of violation. *Human Resource Management International Digest, 8*(6), 28–31.

Pavlou, P. A., & Gefen, D. (2005). Psychological contract violation in online marketplaces: Antecedents, consequences, and moderating role. *Information Systems Research, 16*(4), 372–399.

Ping, Z., Na, L., Scialdone, M. J., & Carey, J. M. (2009). The intellectual movement of human-computer interaction research: A critical assessment of the MIS literature (1990–2008). *AIS Transactions on Human-Computer Interaction, 1*(3), 55–108.

Porter, C. E., & Donthu, N. (2008). Cultivating trust and harvesting value in virtual communities. *Management Science, 54*(1), 113–129.

Porter, M. E. (1979). How competitive forces shape strategy. *Harvard Business Review, 57*(2), 137–145.

Porter, M. E. (2008). The five competitive forces that shape strategy. *Harvard Business Review, 86*(1), 78–93.

Prasso, S. (2010). American made . . . Chinese owned. *Fortune, 161*(7), 84–92.

Pugh, S. D., Skarlicki, D. P., & Passell, B. S. (2003). After the fall: Layoff victims' trust and cynicism in re-employment. *Journal of Occupational and Organizational Psychology, 76*(2), 201–212.

Ragowsky, A., & Gefen, D. (2009). Why information systems management is in trouble and how to save it: A case study in the automotive industry. *Communications of the ACM, 52*(2), 130–133.

Ragowsky, A., Licker, P., & Gefen, D. (2008). Give me information, not technology. *Communications of the ACM, 51*(6), 23–25.

Rai, A., Maruping, L. M., & Venkatesh, V. (2009). Offshore information systems project success: The role of social embeddedness and cultural characteristics. *MIS Quarterly, 33*(3), 617–641.

Ranganathan, C., & Outlay, C. N. (2009). Life after IT outsourcing: Lessons learned from resizing the IT workforce. *MIS Quarterly Executive, 8*(4), 161–173.

Robey, D., & Farrow, D. L. (1982). User involvement in information systems development: A conflict model and empirical test. *Management Science, 28*(1), 73–85.

Robinson, S. L. (1996). Trust and breach of the psychological contract. *Administrative Science Quarterly, 41*(4), 574–599.

Rogers, E. (1967). *Diffusion of innovations.* New York, NY: Free Press.

Rogerson, W. P. (1994). Economic incentives and the defense procurement process. *Journal of Economic Perspectives, 8*, 65–90.

Rousseau, D. M. (1989). Psychological and implied contracts in organizations. *Employee Responsibilities and Rights Journal, 2*, 121–139.

Rustagi, S., King, W. R., & Kirsch, L. J. (2008). Predictors of formal control usage in IT outsourcing partnerships. *Information Systems Research, 19*(2), 126–131.

Salaway, G. (1987). An organizational learning approach to information systems development. *MIS Quarterly, 11*(2), 244–264.

Schneider, I. (2008, June 16). No turning back. *Information Week*, pp. 37–40.

Schneider, I. (2010a, May 13). IBM roadmap earmarks $20 billion for acquisitions. *InformationWeek*. Retrieved from http://www.informationweek.com/news/global-cio/showArticle.jhtml?articleID=224701797&tcss=global-cio

Schneider, I. (2010b, June 26). Top 10 Cloud computing complaints. *InformationWeek*. Retrieved from http://www.informationweek.com/news/software/web_services/showArticle.jhtml?articleID=225701008&cid=nl_IW_cloud_2010-06-30_h

Schrage, M. (2003). Why IT really does matter. *CIO, 16*(20), 30–31

Scott, J. E. (2000). Facilitating interorganizational learning with information technology. *Journal of Management Information Systems, 17*(2), 81–113.

Senor, D., & Singer, S. (2010). *Start-up nation: The story of Israel's economic miricle.* New York, NY: Twelve.

Singh, S. (2001). *The code book.* New York, NY: Random House.

Skarlicki, D. P., & Folger, R. (1997). Retaliation in the Workplace: The roles of distributive, procedural, and interactional justice. *Journal of Applied Psychology, 82*(3), 434–443.

Smick, D. M. (2008). *The world is curved: Hidden dangers to the global economy* New York, NY: Penguin.

Snir, E. M., & Hitt, L. M. (2004). Vendor screening in information technology contracting with a pilot project. *Journal of Organizational Computing and Electronic Commerce, 14*(1), 61–88.

Son, J.-Y., Narasimhan, S., & Riggins, F. J. (2005). Effects of relational factors and channel climate on EDI usage in the customer–supplier relationship. *Journal of Management Information Systems, 22*(1), 321–353.

Szajna, B. (1994). Software evaluation and choice: Predictive validation of the technology acceptance instrument. *MIS Quarterly, 18*(3), 319–324.

Tajfel, H. (1970). Experiments in intergroup discrimination. *Scientific American, 223*(5), 96–102.

Tajfel, H. (1978). Social categorization, social identity and social comparison. In H. Tajfel (Ed.), *Differentiation between social groups* (pp. 61–76). London, England: Academic Press.

Tay, L. (2009, September 11). Qantas project staff get the Big Blues. *iTNews.* Retrieved from http://www.itnews.com.au/News/155428,ibm-qantas-ink -seven-year-outsourcing-deal.aspx

Thomson, S. W. (1883). Electrical units of measurement. *PLA, 1*(1883–05-03).

Tiwana, A., & Keil, M. (2009). Control in internal and outsourced software projects. *Journal of Management Information Systems, 26*(3), 9–44.

Turner, J. C. (1985). Social categorization and the self-concept: A social cognitive theory of group behavior. In E. L. Lawler (Ed.), *Advances in group processes* (Vol. 2, pp. 77–122). London, England: JAI Press.

Tyler, T. R. (1989). The psychology of procedural justice: A test of the group value model. *Journal of Personality and Social Psychology, 57*(5), 830–838.

Watjatrakul, B. (2005). Determinants of IS sourcing decisions: A comparative study of transaction cost theory versus the resource-based view. *Journal of Strategic Information Systems, 14*, 389–415.

Whang, S. (1995). Market provision of custom software: Learning effects and low balling. *Management Science, 41*(8), 1343–1357.

Williamson, O. E. (1979). Transaction cost economics: The governance of contractual relations. *Journal of Law, Economics, and Organization, 11*, 335–361.

Williamson, O. E. (1985). *The economic institutions of capitalism.* New York, NY: Free Press.

Index

A page number followed by an "*f*" refers to a figure on that page.

Announcing the Business Expert Press Digital Library

Concise E-books Business Students Need for Classroom and Research

This book can also be purchased in an e-book collection by your library as

- a one-time purchase,
- that is owned forever,
- allows for simultaneous readers,
- has no restrictions on printing, and
- can be downloaded as PDFs from within the library community.

Our digital library collections are a great solution to beat the rising cost of textbooks. e-books can be loaded into their course management systems or onto student's e-book readers.

The BUSINESS EXPERT PRESS digital libraries are very affordable, with no obligation to buy in future years.

For more information, please visit WWW.BUSINESSEXPERT.COM/LIBRARIES. To set up a trial in the United States, please contact SHERI ALLEN at *sheri.allen@globalepress.com*; for all other regions, contact NICOLE LEE at **NICOLE.LEE@IGROUPNET.COM**.

OTHER TITLES IN OUR INFORMATION SYSTEMS COLLECTION
Series Editors: Daniel Power

Decision Support Basics by Dan Power
Process Mapping and Management by Sue Conger

CPSIA information can be obtained at www.ICGtesting.com
Printed in the USA
236339LV00002B/127/P